Attachment in
Common Sense
and Doodles

A Practical Guide

MIRIAM SILVER

Foreword by Camila Batmanghelidjh

Jessica Kingsley *Publishers*
London and Philadelphia

First published in 2013
by Jessica Kingsley Publishers
116 Pentonville Road
London N1 9JB, UK
and
400 Market Street, Suite 400
Philadelphia, PA 19106, USA

www.jkp.com

Library of Congress Cataloging in Publication Data
Silver, Miriam, 1974-
Attachment in common sense and doodles : a practical guide / Miriam Silver ;
foreword by Camila
Batmanghelidjh.
p. cm.
Includes bibliographical references and index.
ISBN 978-1-84905-314-3 (alk. paper)
1. Attachment behavior in children. 2. Adopted children--Psychology. 3. Abused children--Psychology.
I. Title.
BF723.A75.S55 2013
155.9'2--dc23
2012035329

British Library Cataloguing in Publication Data
A CIP catalogue record for this book is available from the British Library

ISBN 978 1 84905 314 3
eISBN 978 0 85700 624 0

Printed and bound in Great Britain

Contents

Foreword

Britain has been at the forefront of attachment theory. We've given a gift to the world through the theories of Bowlby and Winnicott. The wisdom of attachment theorists have now been further mobilised because neuro-imaging has advanced. Through our scanning machines, we can see the devastation caused structurally and functionally to brains deprived of the tenderness of love. We also know that children with disturbed attachments experience toxic levels of stress which impact their physiological status, making them more vulnerable to illness. The inner world of children with ruptures in attachment is often devastated, chaotic and disturbingly anxious. Attachment deprived children lack a secure base. Their notion of the world is one of a persecutory environment which they relentlessly attempt to survive. These are children whose delusions of mastery are precariously shattered, depleting their self-esteem. How can you be confident of your own competencies when you don't have the confidence that you will be chosen to be loved?

In the absence of the biological carer not being available to provide love and appropriate attachment, how do services mobilise to provide substitute attachments in order to affect reparation and promote development? Attachment is such a big subject: so profound and catalytic, yet so hard to define.

Miriam Silver in *Attachment in Common Sense and Doodles* has taken on the challenge of describing attachment and its potency by breaking it down into bite-size, piercingly clear narratives. She has skillfully woven words, images and doodles in to the fabric of her presentation, consequently producing one of the most accessible narratives I have seen on the subject of attachment.

Her considerable experience as a clinician comes through. She doesn't make recommendations that are pie in the sky. Instead, her techniques are realistic, clearly well practiced and intelligently selected. So I hope you'll pick up *Attachment in Common Sense and Doodles* and enjoy the grin that will take over your face as you marvel at how cleverly you've been taken step by step through the attachment journey. Surely there's nothing more wonderful than seeing some grand and potentially nebulous theory be so well packaged into bite-size chunks. Enjoy one of the most delicious intellectually informed clinical thought meals you're going to have in your life. It did the trick. This book is definitely my attachment security blanket.

Camila Batmanghelidjh
Psychotherapist, and founder of
The Place2Be and Kids Company
London, UK

Acknowledgements

Thanks must first go to my own attachment figures: my wonderful husband, my parents, my children (who have made me do this stuff myself); and to the colleagues I work with at LifePsychol and Evolving Families.

The material in this book was devised whilst I was running groups for adoptive and foster carers in Northamptonshire. Their feedback, along with comments from colleagues and professionals I have trained, helped the content to evolve and encouraged me to write this book, as I was often asked whether I could provide some more detailed information that people could take away to read up in more depth or share with others who were unable to attend the group.

I have also been inspired by attending training, including doing Level One and Level Two of Dan Hughes' training in Dyadic Developmental Psychotherapy, workshops with Kim Golding, and with Todd and Melissa Nichols of the Family Attachment Narrative Centre. Finally I have been involved in running the British Psychological Society network for Clinical Psychologists working with Looked After and Adopted Children (CPLAAC) where I have met many of my peers who are delivering clinical services for and working with populations of children who are looked after and adopted all across the United Kingdom. This has been a great chance to share good practice, keep abreast of the latest research and network with those who have written books that have inspired me in my practice.

Preface

This book is intended for foster carers and adoptive parents, kinship carers, social workers and anyone else who is dealing with children who have been placed away from their birth parents to grow up after having experienced early trauma, neglect or abuse.

My aim is to explain in common sense terms what might be going on for those children and some things that might be useful to do when helping them make the most of the new parenting they are experiencing and to move on with their lives.

There are many excellent books out there that give much more technical and detailed explanations of attachment theory and different forms of therapeutic models (and there are references and further reading at the end so that you can choose to read some of them if you want) but they are often overly complex and not suitable for the lay reader. This book, however, is designed to explain in simple and practical terms the key concepts and how to apply them in real life. I've tried to write in a way that should not be difficult to read and which does not require any previous reading or specialist knowledge to make sense. I've tried to share some examples from my own life and from people with whom I have worked[1] to illustrate each idea and apply

1   The case examples I have used are composite cases. They are anonymised examples made up from several people I have worked with so that they reflect a typical case, rather than one particular individual.

it to real life. Most of all, the book should be relevant to the children you are looking after.

It might help you to know a little bit about my background to help you understand my qualifications and how I came to write the book. I am a consultant clinical psychologist and for the past 15 years I have specialised in working with children and families who have experienced adversity. I've taken a particular interest in working with children who live outside their family of origin, such as children who are in foster care, in adoptive families or living with extended family members, and young people who live in residential placements. I've read a lot of books and scientific papers about attachment, therapy and the impact of trauma and abuse, and I've conducted my own research in this area, presenting and publishing this as much as I can (although there is still much I'd like to write about).

I've been one of a small but growing group of professionals who have developed specialist expertise in working with attachment relationships and looked after and adopted children, both leading an NHS team and acting as an expert witness in the family courts.

My career has given me quite a rounded viewpoint of the experiences that lead young people to become looked after and adopted (e.g. the abuse, neglect and chaotic care that many of them have been through in their lives before the orders were passed and they were moved to different homes) as well as understanding the court process, and the outcomes for them living in their new homes. Working to support looked after and adopted children therapeutically, I have also encountered the kind of difficulties that come up for foster and adoptive carers and have had the privilege of working alongside some of those people to help them form the best possible relationships with their children.

I started out mainly doing consultations for individual families, where I would meet the professionals and the foster/adoptive parents and we would talk about the challenges they faced. It struck me that even though their stories were each unique, and their children at different ages and presenting different challenges, many people were experiencing similar types of issues. I ended up often using the same diagrams or 'doodles' which feature within this book to explain ideas to many different families. Because of that, I developed and ran a group that I designed called Managing Behaviour with Attachment in Mind to teach foster and adoptive parents about some of the issues that recurrently came up in consultation.

While many books have been written about attachment, it's my intention for this book to provide a fresh approach by presenting the information in an accessible form. To achieve this, I tried to avoid technical terminology and to be practical, accessible and concise, with numerous doodles to translate information into visual form.

While trying to keep things simple, I've also included signposts for readers who are interested in finding out more. Within the text, there are some numbered references to related academic papers. Brief details of these are listed at the bottom of the page to enable you to find them in the reference list at the end of the book. An Appendix summarises the impact of early trauma, abuse and neglect. At the end of the book I've also included additional reading, along with a glossary of terms, although I have provided explanations within the text when the terms are first introduced.

I hope this book of words and doodles offers you plenty to look at and to think about, and that you'll try some of the activities which feature.

CHAPTER 1

What Is Attachment and Why Does It Matter?

Attachment is the nature of a relationship with someone who you love or rely on or whose opinions are important to you. Usually the primary attachment is between a baby and their parent(s) and it begins before that baby is even born and continues throughout their lives. However, you do not usually just have one attachment relationship; you probably have many (this might include your parents, your carers, your grandparents, your teachers, your neighbours, your friends, your partners, your children, or other family members) but the first relationships you have often set the template for how other relationships develop.[2]

If your primary carer forms a 'secure base' then the child learns to use that person as a base from which to explore the world. A 'secure base' when it comes to parenting a baby is someone who cares about them and who is physically there and interested in the messages that the baby is giving them. They are fairly calm and predictable, do not harm the baby and are not so preoccupied with their own problems (e.g. depression, domestic violence, drug misuse, alcohol, mental health problems, relationships, work, social media) that they aren't reliably available to interact with the baby. A secure base gives the baby the

---

2   Attachment has categories and impacts on other relationships. See Ainsworth *et al.* (1978).

best chance to learn about themselves, other people and the world in a positive way. It is associated with numerous positive outcomes for the infant, which last throughout that child's life and makes them more likely to be able to replicate a similar positive experience for their own children if they later become a parent themselves.

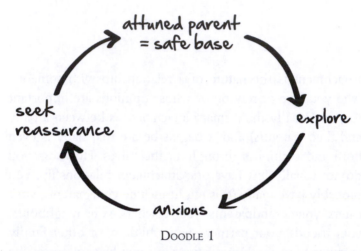

DOODLE 1

As you can see from Doodle 1, a secure base allows the child to learn about the world in a cycle that repeats many times every day. The child leaves the secure base and goes to explore, the exploring makes them anxious and so they seek reassurance by returning to their secure base. One example of that might be when children first come to see me in my clinic (which is similar to what you might have noticed when you have taken a child anywhere new). They might come holding their parent's hand or clinging on to their leg and the new environment might be a bit scary – particularly meeting lots of new people – so they might hide behind the parent until they feel a bit more settled and the parent's body language has given them signals that it is safe to go and have a look at the toys in my room. As they begin to settle they might gradually go and look at the toys but will keep a close watch on the signals their parent is giving. Then I might start talking about the difficulties that have been happening in the family and the child might become a bit more anxious and return to hide behind their parent for a while, seeking reassurance by returning to their safe base. This cycle might repeat several times during an appointment but it might repeat a hundred times or more during a day in which a parent is interacting with a baby or a young child.

Even as an adult I continue to use my secure bases. So, for example, if I were to have a sudden rash or illness I might want to find out about it, so I might look it up on Google or I might book a doctor's appointment. That might make me anxious and therefore I would want to speak to someone who makes me feel secure, like my husband or my parents, in order to feel better before I could then go out and deal with those stresses head on.

When that person who is a secure base is available to the child, predictable and safe, then that cycle leads the child to form what we call a secure attachment pattern. That pattern helps them form healthy, mutually respectful relationships with others throughout their lives, and to build a good self-image, social skills and empathy. Secure infants learn to recognise and regulate their emotions and to recognise which behaviours please their carers and are socially rewarded. Research has shown that secure attachment goes on to be a significant protective factor against a wide range of difficulties. For example, we know that people with secure attachments go on to generally do better at school, in the work place, in their relationships, in parenting and also in their physical health (see the Appendix).

However, not every child is lucky enough to have a parent who can offer a secure base. Some parents are physically or emotionally unavailable for one reason or another. Perhaps they are so depressed that they spend a lot of time zoned out, or they have serious learning disabilities that mean it is harder for them to be sensitive to the needs of the child. Maybe there are major physical or sensory disabilities, or maybe they are misusing drugs or alcohol. It may be that they are physically not there (interacting with the child) very much because they are working long hours and the quality of childcare is very poor, or they are constantly multi-tasking with addictive levels of gambling, internet use, computer games, emails/texts, etc. or they are preoccupied with other stresses in their lives (such as family conflict, domestic violence, harassment, debt, etc.). It may be that they have formed a view that a child is too demanding and have disengaged from them, or because they think that putting a child in their room or sitting them in front of the television all day is sufficient parenting. But for whatever reason, even though they do nothing actively harmful to the child (at least not to the extent of physical or sexual abuse), they are not able to notice and sensitively respond to the signals that their child is giving to them frequently enough to offer that secure base.[3]

If that is the case, then, as you can see from Doodle 2, the child learns one of two patterns to cope with that situation. They may learn to explore and explore and keep on exploring, denying that there is any anxiety (because no reassurance is available) until they become overly self-sufficient and seem fearless and autonomous beyond their years. Or they do the opposite and constantly seek

---

3   Some parents are not attuned to a baby's signals (e.g. due to mental health, learning difficulty, or preoccupation with other things). See Cleaver, Unell, and Aldgate (1999) and Reder and Lucey (2000).

reassurance but never feel reassured (because the reassurance is not effective) and so become very clingy and dependent.

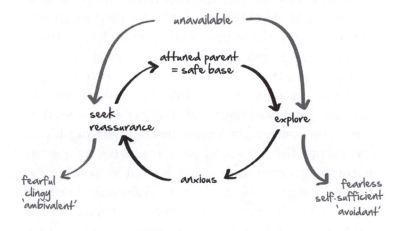

DOODLE 2

Children in that fearless and overly self-sufficient group can often seem mature beyond their years. They can be quiet, undemanding and may be quite rejecting of nurture and fearless about things that are dangerous in the world. They may either present as needing very little adult care or may end up so fearless and tough that they are considered 'beyond parental control'. In attachment terminology those children are known as 'insecure avoidant' – they avoid attachment relationships because they are not accustomed to being able to use the secure base for reassurance.

On the other hand, when a child goes the other way and becomes very clingy they will often present as immature and needy. They constantly seek the reassurance and nurture they require but because the parent is unable to provide this secure base, they do not feel reassured enough to be able to do the normal process of exploring. The parent is perhaps too anxious, depressed or too intrusive to allow the child sufficient autonomy to explore so the child learns to be dependent, immature and needy. In attachment terminology these children are referred to as 'insecure ambivalent' because they want their attachment relationships to reassure them but they do not feel reassured.

Both being 'avoidant' and being 'ambivalent' are sensible, consistent patterns for dealing with the type of attachment figure that a child has experienced and they are quite widespread in the general population. These two patterns are called 'insecure but organised', attachments. They are not as protective as having a secure attachment relationship but they are not as damaging as the final category of attachment relationship ('insecure disorganised', described in the next paragraph), because the parent is at least fairly consistent and not actively harmful, so the child can at least learn ways of dealing with the world that gain a predictable response. Therefore, although these relationships are not following the ideal template, they should not be automatically seen as harmful or pathological, as they are relatively prevalent and not outside the range of normal relationships. However, within each category there is a range of presentations, and the less there has been a secure attachment figure available and the greater the other needs of the child (e.g. if they also have some learning disability or a neurodevelopmental disorder) the more likely that child is to need additional support in order to thrive.

The final category involves parents who provide care that is chaotic, unpredictable or at times harmful towards the child. This would include any parents who are physically, sexually or emotionally abusive or chronically neglectful to an extent that endangers the child. It would also include parents who are so busy surviving their own chaotic lives, filled with substance abuse and/or domestic violence and/or conflict and stress, that the child's needs take low priority and the child is exposed to the chaotic, conflict-ridden environment that surrounds them. Children in this category are known as 'insecure disorganised' because no single 'organised' strategy would help them to feel safe the way it does in the organised insecure patterns. As you can see from Doodle 3, they therefore learn to make the best of each situation, treating each adult differently to get their needs met. This might lead children like this to be described as manipulative, false, provocative or superficially charming (particularly to those other than their main attachment figure).

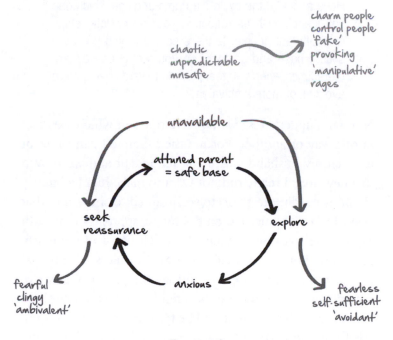

DOODLE 3

These strategies make sense in the context of their lives. So if, for example, a stranger is more likely to give a child food or attention or comfort than their parent, they would learn to approach strangers in a way that is likely to get their needs met, either by being charming or by being babyish or by trying to meet the needs of the adult in some way that they would reward. Similarly, if it is hard to get any attention in your environment you learn to do things that cannot be ignored, the things that really press people's buttons. All of these strategies are adaptive responses to abnormal experiences and make the child extremely vulnerable.[4]

Reflection: Spotting your own patterns now

Have a look at the cycle diagrams and see which one you identify with as reflecting your own relationships with different people. Is there someone you use as a secure base and go to when you feel stressed? Are there times when you feel pushed towards being more avoidant or more ambivalent?

Normally under stress we all have times in which we react in one way or another. For me the example I can think of is when my husband was made redundant and we moved to a new area. I really did not want to make him feel guilty about us needing to relocate so I wanted to show him that everything was fine. I didn't want to approach him with my stresses because it would have felt like I was unfairly burdening him at a difficult time. So I would smile and act like everything was fine. I would say things like 'Oh, we're moving away from the area where I know lots of people to a new area? That's fine; it will be for the best. I'm changing job from a job where I know everybody and I know my

---

4   Disorganised attachment is a normal response to abuse and has poor outcomes. See Carlson *et al.* (1989), Van IJzendoorn *et al.* (1999) and Zeanah, Keyes and Settles (2003).

routines and I'm enjoying everything that I do, to a place where everything will be different? That's fine, don't worry. We're moving in to a house that needs doing up and has no kitchen, bathroom or central heating yet? That's fine, don't worry, it'll be a fun project.' So I started a new job, in a new town, in a new house, without the support of my friends and family around, and denied the emotional impact of that. I put on a good show and didn't burden anyone with guilt or moaning. I wore a smiley face, and carried on being a competent psychologist and a supportive wife, and I kept all those negative feelings to myself. This is an example of avoidant attachment style under stress.

I realised after about a year that only showing one facet of my feelings to the people around me meant that all my relationships felt insincere and lacking in depth and I began to be more honest with people. It was reassuring to know that they didn't crumble under the additional stress I placed upon them and my relationships grew back to being as strong and secure as they had always felt. It was a very helpful learning experience for me because it now helps me to empathise more effectively with those children who have come from one home to another and who are trying to present a pleasing but slightly false feeling persona so that they are liked in the new placement; it is something we will come back to later.

Reflection: Spotting your own childhood patterns

Now think about your own childhood relationships and whether there was anyone around who led you to feel less secure or who treated you badly. What impact do you think that has had on you? What made the impact more or less significant for you?

When it comes to attachment relationships, particularly friendships and romantic partners, we tend to seek out people with a similar or complementary attachment style to ourselves. Those first formative relationships are important in setting the template for the relationships that will follow. For example, it is common in my experience for anxious, dependent people to pair up with someone strong but avoidant. If you have a secure base during childhood then you are able to seek out people who will form positive, respectful, mutually beneficial relationships. But we all come across people who are chaotic and harmful and carry a disorganised attachment pattern, so it can be that we have a mixture of attachment styles influencing our lives at different times. Where those relationships are transitory or happen later in your life you can normally recognise them as negative relationships and avoid them, keeping your main template of relationships as the ones that are more secure. We know from research that where there is any one secure relationship in a person's childhood this is incredibly protective, even where other relationships are insecure (even insecure disorganised).

Having a primary attachment relationship which is an insecure disorganised relationship is something that can have a profound effect. Children who are classified as having insecure disorganised attachment styles do much worse in all kinds of biological, psychological and social outcomes. That is, they tend to do worse in school and later on in employment, they have a higher risk of substance abuse or involvement in crime, more risk of relationship breakdown, more difficulties with parenting and risk of their own children being taken into care, more risk of mental health problems and even more risk of physical problems such as cancer, heart disease and diabetes. There are clinicians and researchers who would argue that almost all challenging behaviour seen in the home and the school relates to poor early care and attachment experiences.[5]

	General	In Care
secure	50–60%	> 10% ?
organised but insecure	30–40%	40% ?
disorganised insecure	10%	50% ?

DOODLE 4

When thinking about attachment categories the one thing that I did not mention earlier is the percentages of people in the general population who fall into the different categories. As you can see from Doodle 4, studies generally say that around 50 per cent of people are in the secure category, around 40 per cent are in the insecure but organised categories and around 10 per cent are in the insecure disorganised category, though this really varies from study to study depending on the population, the age at which it is measured and the methodology.[6]

However, it is worth noticing that children in the Care system are very skewed in this distribution; it seems very unlikely that there are significant numbers of children in the secure category because by definition children in the Care system have had separation from their first caregivers and have often been through neglect or abuse and multiple changes of placement. From my experience working with looked after and adopted children during the past decade

---

5   Trauma underlies most of disruptive behaviour. See Dodge, Bates and Pettit (1990), Sansone, Furukhi and Wiederman (2012) and Wolfe *et al.* (2003).

6   Proportions of children in the attachment categories in the general population. See van IJzendoorn *et al.* (1999).

and my understanding of the research literature, I would suggest it is probably pretty much a reverse pattern of what you see in the general population.

Based on research with children exposed to trauma, under 10 per cent of looked after children are securely attached at the point that they arrive in a new placement, around 40 per cent of children arriving in placement are insecure but organised and around 50 per cent of children would reach that disorganised category.[7] The prevalence of the more dysfunctional attachment patterns is not surprising because looked after and adopted children make up less than 1 per cent of children and are only taken from the 1 per cent of families in the wider population where there has been the most disruptive and damaging experiences going on around them.

There is also the question of diagnosis, as some clinicians will diagnose 'Attachment Disorder' in a particular child, or use the controversial label of 'Reactive Attachment Disorder'. I tend to avoid these labels as I do not believe that it is a disorder that can be identified in the child as an individual in isolation. Attachment disorder is a pattern that plays out between that child and the people around them, particularly their primary caregiver(s). I also think that it is very important that the label does not imply that there is an organic underlying condition the child was born with, as I see attachment disorder as being a normal response to abnormal circumstances and not something innate in the child. As such I tend to favour Bessel van der Kolk's view of Chronic Developmental Trauma as a subcategory of post-traumatic stress.[8]

---

7   Proportions in different attachment categories amongst traumatised/looked after children. See van IJzendoorn *et al.* (1999).
8   Chronic developmental trauma. See van der Kolk (2005).

CHAPTER 2

Can Attachment Patterns Change?

It is incredible to think what a profound effect the parenting you receive in the first two years of life can have, and on such a wide-ranging number of outcomes (a brief summary of the impact of poor early care is given in the Appendix, complete with references to some of the scientific studies). We also know that the longer a child is left in a chaotic home without secure attachment relationships, the more difficult it is to change the patterns later and the more challenging it becomes to help that child get onto a better trajectory for their adult relationships.[9]

However, even children whose primary relationship is insecure disorganised do not inevitably go on to have that attachment pattern for life. In fact there is a significant group of adults who, when studied, have a fifth attachment classification known as 'earned secure' (or 'learned secure'). These individuals have used other relationships in their life to recognise and reflect that the pattern they have learnt from their parents is not the only one available, and was not the quality of care that they deserved or want to replicate. They have been able to use a secure base in later life to learn how to become one themselves.[10] That learning

---

9 The longer a child is left in chaos/trauma the harder it is to recover. See Felitti *et al.* (1998) and Glaser (2001).
10 Earned secure attachment. See Saunders *et al.* (2011).

experience can be from one consistent caregiver during childhood, a foster or adoptive parent, a close friendship, an adult relationship or even the therapeutic relationship with a counsellor or psychologist or other professional in the mental health sector that they have seen over an extended period of time. That is why hope is not lost even when someone has had an awful start in life, and it is so valuable when people recognise their own difficulties and seek out the right support in order to think about and change their own attachment pattern to a more organised or secure one.

The people in the 'earned secure' category can go on to be quite resilient in their parenting and their relationships; nearly as much so as the people who had secure relationships in their childhood to begin with.[11] This represents a powerful message of hope because it means that anybody can change their attachment style and there is never a point at which it is too late to change, though obviously the earlier the better. There are increasing numbers of therapists who are able to recognise and work with children and adults whose early care and attachment experiences have been poor, in order to help them develop these 'earned secure' qualities, and challenge their patterns of thinking and behaviour. This can enable them to form healthier relationships and a more positive sense of themselves, others and the world.

One of the things that predicts whether you will be an optimal parent who can ensure your child is secure is your ability to recognise the links between childhood experiences and the kind of person that child becomes later in their life.[12] Generally people who say, 'I was smacked all the time and it didn't do me any harm' haven't really

---

11   Earned secure outcomes are nearly equivalent to secure. See Lichtenstein Phelps, Belsky and Crnic (1998).

12   The importance of reflective functioning in parenting. See Fonagy, Steele and Steele (1991) and Slade (2005).

reflected on their own experiences as much as would really be necessary to draw that conclusion.

In my therapeutic work I've met children and adults with a multitude of different responses to the trauma and neglect they have experienced in their life. Some adults are incredibly worried about their ability to parent, and how to do the job of parenting differently to the parenting that they experienced in their own childhood. I view that anxiety as a good sign! Being concerned about how to parent as well as your child deserves is really natural and something most people experience at some point. This is true even for people who have had great upbringings and who have given birth to children who don't have any difficulties. If you have experienced adversity, then it's a really positive sign to be actively thinking about how to do something different, and how to not keep following the patterns that are familiar. It is this active reflection that leads people to becoming more secure and able to provide better care and more emotional attunement to their children than they experienced themselves. However, it's hard work to consciously parent your children differently to how you grew up, compared with simply following the familiar patterns formed by the way you were parented!

The parents who cause me concern are the ones where it is clear that they had very poor care in their own childhood, but they have later come to accept, normalise or even idealise this. They describe their childhoods as being happy and their parents as being caring and loving, even when the evidence shows they were abused and neglected. It is this (perhaps unconscious) desire to squash out the negative memories of the past, to downgrade the importance of their unhappy feelings and whitewash over problems that suggests these parents do not recognise the shortcomings in their own experience and are thus not able to reflect on how they need to improve things and can end up repeating familiar patterns.

CASE EXAMPLE: A worthless man

I recently spoke to a man whose partner wanted them to try for a baby. He felt that he would 'never be ready to be a father'. He reported feeling 'depressed, useless and a failure' all of his adult life. He said that other people perceived him as either distant or angry but that he was simply responding to perceived criticism as he thought they looked down on him. He told me that he desperately wanted to be loved but that his girlfriend and prior partners found him 'too emotional but in all the wrong ways'. He thought this had nothing to do with his childhood, which he said was 'fine' and 'as good as anyone else's' and 'not an excuse for my failure'.

As we formed a greater level of trust, I learned that his parents were domestically violent throughout his childhood, and he was frequently criticised as a young boy, particularly when he expressed any needs or showed any distress. He had learned that responding with anger to parental criticism made him feel stronger and less vulnerable, and to emotionally shut off and detach himself from others. Although he still felt worthless inside he had learnt to hide this behind a façade of not caring, or when pressed, his anger. He was sceptical that anyone could find anything lovable about him, and struggled to really trust anyone else with his feelings. The idea of having a baby was terrifying to him, as a baby would have needs he would be expected to fulfil and he did not feel able to provide the care necessary. We worked on using our therapeutic relationship as a model of trust and being valued to help build his self-image.

CASE EXAMPLE: A soft mother

I recently worked with a mother who was having difficulties providing any boundaries and structure for her child. She found it really difficult to set any rules or demonstrate any consequences if the child failed to follow her instructions. Because of this the child's behaviour was quite disruptive and oppositional, and the school had to involve their behaviour and inclusion *team in an effort to stop the child from being excluded from mainstream lessons.*

When we explored the mother's history it emerged that she had been physically abused by her step-father and her mother had been very 'soft' with her to compensate for this, but had never intervened to protect the children. The lady had learnt that there were only two ways to parent – being punitive and abusive or being soft and ineffective, and she did not want to be the former. We worked together to see that there was plenty of scope for middle ground between these two extremes, and that the best parents are able to provide some boundaries and consequences to help to shape a child's behaviour and prepare them for functioning well in the world. Setting limits for her children did not make her similar to her father.

Being a parent is a huge responsibility because you are shaping the life of a person. For many people, when they have a child and feel how overwhelming that responsibility is, their views about parenting change a lot. They feel huge amounts of guilt when they think that they haven't got it right for the vulnerable little person who is totally dependent on them and who they love more than they ever thought possible. However, for most caring parents, the standards they believe they should aspire to are much closer to perfection than is required. Provided that you are able to love a child, see them as an individual, give them positive feedback and offer them developmentally appropriate stimulation, you are likely to be doing a good job.

However, the aim of this book is to help you fine tune those intuitive (and perhaps well practised) parenting skills to meet the needs of children who have experienced early trauma and poor care. The demands of 're-parenting' such children are much greater than of parenting a birth child who has not experienced such stressors.[13] Hopefully the

---

13   See Appleyard and Osofsky (2003) and Banyard, Rozelle and England (2001).

rest of the book will help you think about what is different about children who have experienced abuse, neglect and chaotic or harmful early care, and what you can do to assist such children to recover from those experiences and go on to be healthy, happy young people who form successful relationships with others.

The first challenge, however, is to recognise the attachment patterns that your child brings with them, and to gently act in a way that brings them towards your secure pattern (and to seek help and support if you ever feel pulled out of your secure pattern). To do this we need to work out what the child's underlying need is as well as the expressed need. For example, a child who has an ambivalent attachment style will strongly express their need for reassurance, but they may need to be given a message that it is okay to learn to explore. On the other hand, a child who is avoidant will seem self-sufficient and will explore but won't be keen to return to have reassurance and nurture. But this unexpressed need being met is what will help them to become more secure, so it will be beneficial for them if you can find ways to offer reassurance and comfort, even when they don't ask for this overtly.

If the child is insecure disorganised, then it might be that they present different needs to different people, or express their needs in very dysfunctional and indirect ways. The most helpful strategy might be to begin to name the needs that are being expressed so that they are acknowledged directly, and to offer a level of consistency and understanding they have not experienced before. For example, it might be that you can say, 'I think you are feeling a bit worried about this' even if they are showing difficult behaviour rather than anxiety in a new situation. Whatever the child's pattern is, it is really useful to have a think about both the expressed and unexpressed needs, so that you are not unintentionally reinforcing unhelpful patterns (see Golding 2008).

MEASURING EARLY ATTACHMENT

Researchers can reliably pick up which attachment category children fall into by 12 months of age by putting them through the Strange Situation task.[14] The researchers observe how the infants respond to separation from their parent and what they do when they are reunified. What is amazing about attachment is that it isn't a quality of an individual in isolation. The components of that infant's personality, or any organic conditions they might have, affect their attachment pattern remarkably little. We know this because attachment does not magically appear when the child appears, complete with their personal characteristics.[15] Researchers can do the Adult Attachment Interview with expectant mothers during pregnancy, and by talking to them and hearing about their ways of understanding the world they can already predict which kind of attachment style the child is going to have in two thirds of cases. This is really important because it tells us something about the fact that attachment is not innate in a child; it is a response to their experiences and their relationships. This also gives us clues about attachment patterns being transmitted from generation to generation.

One of the things that we know from studying the attachment classifications of parents and the subsequent attachment patterns of their children is that when you have parents who have experienced poor care themselves, they are much more likely to go on and re-create a similar attachment style (or an equally dysfunctional attachment

---

14   See Ainsworth *et al.* (1978).
15   See Fonagy *et al.* (1991) and van IJzendoorn (1995).

style) with their children.[16] What is interesting, however, is that it is not completely fixed and continues to respond to the experiences and relationships you have throughout life. So if someone 'inherits' a reasonable attachment template from a parent whose attachment style was organised insecure (which is quite common and not pathological), that person might get into a relationship that then somehow goes downhill (e.g. because there is some drug use or domestic violence or the partner's mental health deteriorates). That might gradually undermine their self-image more and more until they are functioning in a very chaotic way. If they have a baby at this point, their child may then be insecure disorganised and therefore do worse in attachment terms than the parent's attachment experience would suggest.

Equally, however, it may be that parents who have come out of very destructive patterns, and as children had very insecure or disorganised attachment patterns, can come away and reflect on that later and form more stable relationships into which they have a child. Or they might have one protective relationship with a teacher, neighbour or grandparent who models for them a more secure pattern that they can then draw on as a parent. Or they might as an adult seek therapy and the therapist might provide that secure relationship, or a sounding board against which to test out the thoughts, feelings, behaviours and beliefs that they have learnt from early life. In any of these scenarios they may go on, despite this very difficult background, to be able to parent in a much more secure way. As I mentioned above, in attachment research we call those people earned secure (or learned secure).

---

16   Parents' attachment styles influence the infants' attachment style. See van IJzendoorn, Juffer and Duyvesteyn (1995).

A lot of research literature shows that people who are in the earned secure group actually do nearly as well at parenting as people whose childhoods gave them a secure classification in the first place. In my view, when you look at secure versus earned secure, people who are in the earned secure category are very resilient as they are used to challenges and overcoming them, but have more buttons to press from their own history. On the other hand, people who are in the secure category may have had a very quiet, easy life and not have been confronted by those challenges. This means they may not have acquired the level of resilience of those in the earned secure group, but out of all the attachment groups they have the strongest innate pattern and the fewest buttons to press that could affect their parenting.

In my experience (supported by several research studies), adoptive and foster parents and care professionals often fall into either the secure or earned secure groups,[17] but which one of these it is gives them different characteristics. So it is quite interesting to look at how those patterns work and think about where you fit in. As I said earlier, you can probably recognise yourself in bits of these descriptions and it is good to reflect on what patterns you bring to the relationship as this increases your resilience. It is also worth remembering that under stress we can all tip one way or the other, even if we are secure. It is well known for example that health concerns, employment changes such as redundancy, relationship breakdown and other major life events make people less secure, though this change is normally temporary.[18]

---

17   See Caltabiano and Thorpe (2007).
18   Attachment style changes under stress (e.g. with infertility or if in a domestic violence relationship). See Burns (1990), Hart and McMahon (2006), McMahon *et al.* (1999) and Rothman (1986).

When you think about who goes on to become earned secure, research highlights certain qualities which are associated with that;[19] one is being the kind of person that reflects a lot on life. I think that sometimes it is an intuitive thing and sometimes it is learnt from the people around you. Being intelligent is quite protective because it lets you reflect and observe that things are different in other families. But also having models somewhere in your life repertoire of what secure relationships are like is very protective; so no matter how chaotic your life is, if you have one or two good relationships your outcomes are almost always better than if you have only had negative disruptive relationships.[20] This is why it is so important that we acknowledge and give credit to the fact that a teacher's relationship, or a neighbour's or a grandparent's relationship, and definitely a foster carer or adoptive parent, can actually turn around a child's life. One secure attachment relationship can be amazingly powerful.

Reflection: Recognising attachment styles

Try to think about your own attachment relationships and what has influenced your attachment style over time. When have you been more or less secure? Now think about the child you care for. What may have influenced his or her attachment style? How would you wish to influence it? What barriers might there be in doing this?

---

19   Earned secure is related to intelligence, reflective functioning or other qualities of the individual. See Fonagy *et al.* (1994) and Saunders *et al.* (2011).
20   See Gass, Jenkins, and Dunn (2007) and Werner and Smith (1992).

CHAPTER 3

What Is 'Good Enough' Care, and What Does It Do?

A good carer can provide a safe and reasonably predictable environment in which to bring up their baby. They give the baby enough attention to notice the signals the baby communicates when feeling hungry, tired, has wind, is unwell, or has done a wee or poo in their nappy and will try to resolve that by providing appropriate food, rest, burping, appropriate treatment, and keeping them clean and changing their nappy. A good carer will notice the temperature and check that the baby is appropriately dressed or covered. They will provide soothing movements and skin contact by cradling, cuddling, rocking, stroking or patting, along with talking or singing to the baby in order to help calm them if they are distressed or soothe them to sleep if they are tired. They will interact with the baby in a way that is engaging and stimulating but at an appropriate level to the baby's development. The food they provide will also be tailored to the baby's developmental stage and their individual needs. The clothing they provide will fit comfortably and be kept relatively clean. They will wash the baby sufficiently frequently, and be observant to any signs of ill health.

Importantly, they will recognise psychological and emotional need as well as providing physical care. They will take pleasure in interacting with the baby and show that they care about the baby. They will allow the developing infant to explore within a safe and reasonably clean environment, and be careful to ensure that other people who interact with the baby will do so safely and in a way that doesn't cause the baby distress. They will give the baby enough time with a limited group of (typically one to four) specific individuals so that the baby can start to recognise them and form relationships. And as the infant starts to develop, a good carer will help them to recognise their own feelings by naming them, and recognise the feelings of others by exaggerating their own facial expressions and vocal tone when expressing feelings towards the infant. They will give the infant increasing autonomy and provide a variety of experiences to encourage developing social confidence.

We can think of all of these experiences as bricks in the wall of experiences required for healthy development (see Doodle 5). Amazingly these simple and frequently intuitive ways to care for a baby are all that it takes to help the baby's brain develop, and for their map of the world to be formed on the basis that they are a lovable individual, that other people are generally good, and the world is an interesting and mainly safe place to live.[21] This is the basis of a secure attachment and optimal development.

When I talk about this to parents or carers, they often feel that they fall short of the mark, and worry that they need to respond to every signal from the baby correctly first time, every single time. Actually the research evidence doesn't show that such perfection is required. From what I've read I'd say that, provided the baby's basic care needs are met, 'good enough care' equates to understanding the baby's signals and responding to them appropriately at least one third of the time,[22] so most people who worry

---

21   Good care leads to adaptive and positive core beliefs. See Wearden *et al.* (2008).
22   'Good enough' parenting isn't perfect. See Hoghughi and Speight (1998), Tronick (1986) and Winnicott (1953, 1965).

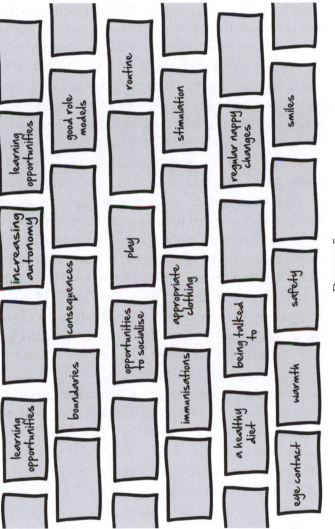

learning opportunities • increasing autonomy • learning opportunities • good role models • boundaries • consequences • routine • play • opportunities to socialise • stimulation • appropriate clothing • immunisations • regular nappy changes • being talked to • a healthy diet • smiles • safety • warmth • eye contact

DOODLE 5

about this are probably managing it just fine. If you are attempting to help a child catch up for missed experiences, compensate for abuse and/or poor early care and/or changes of placement and change the patterns they have already formed, then even if you want to be really ambitious this means you should aim to get the message and respond sensitively at least two thirds of the time. That's a lot easier to aim for than one hundred per cent, and it means that you can be a great parent even if you are sometimes tired or grouchy or need to do the cooking or go to the toilet rather than interacting with the child at that moment.

There are lots of reasons why a caregiver may not be able to offer attuned care to an infant. As I've already mentioned, they might be physically unavailable because they are simply not around the baby enough for some reason and they leave the child alone (e.g. in their bedroom or in front of the television) or in poor quality care. It may be that they are constantly multi-tasking with addictive levels of gambling, internet use, computer games, emails/texts, etc. or they are preoccupied with other stresses in their lives (such as family conflict, domestic violence, harassment, debt, etc.). It may be that they have formed a view that a child is too demanding and have disengaged from them because of their own avoidant templates of how to relate to others. Or they might be emotionally unavailable due to their own mental health or attachment history. They might have physical or sensory disabilities that make it harder to care for a child without support, or serious learning disabilities that mean it is harder to recognise the needs of the child. Maybe they are using drugs or alcohol to an extent that means they are unable to offer coherent and consistent care. They might be simply surviving themselves if there is a high level of conflict around, or they are in a war zone, or living below the poverty line (e.g. as illegal immigrants). The child may have lost a parent to suicide, or may have been abandoned or handed round to other members of the family. Each of these scenarios would have a different impact on a child.

Reflection: Your child's experiences

Have a think about what you know of the story that applies to your child or children. Would they have received good quality care at any point? Would the care have fallen below 'good enough' at any point? What might the experience have been like of growing up in that environment? Don't be surprised if this brings you strong feelings of sadness or anger. These are a sign of your empathy for your child, and are important to think about, as they reflect the emotions that the child may need to go through to grieve their losses as they become apparent to them.

Whatever the cause might be, I think it is worth thinking further about what happens when care is not 'good enough'. The first thing that happens is that the child does not get all the right experience bricks for their early development (see Doodle 6). There are gaps where the child should have had the experiences that teach them the components of social skills, and provide a positive self-image and resilience. This is something we will come back to. Secondly, when the child is exposed to a chaotic or threatening environment (such as when caregivers are shouting at each other, or intoxicated, or sometimes hurt, mistreat or shout at the baby) this has a huge impact on them, which we will come back to when we think about brain development and the fight or flight instinct. The way the body and the brain work and the impact of experience on this will be the subject of the next chapter.

increasing autonomy

learning opportunities

boundaries

opportunities to socialise

play

appropriate clothing

being talked to

warmth

DOODLE 6

But first let's think a little more about attunement and 'good enough' care. When we think about what you would hope that a parent would provide for a child in their day-to-day care, you can list a huge number of things that I see as building blocks for their development. You might want to try this activity.

✎ Activity: Brick walls

✦ Often in my groups I set people the task of writing lists of what 'good enough' parenting looks like for a 0–6-month-old, or a 6–12-month-old, or a pre-schooler, or a primary-school-aged child, or an older child. What are the things at each age that the child will have or experience if their care is good enough? The things we write on the bricks might be as simple as having a safe environment, immunisations, having enough sleep, having shelter, having warmth, healthy food, sufficient hygiene, having someone meet your medical needs, having someone change your nappy regularly, having someone smile at you, having someone come when you cry, experiencing being sung to, being smiled at, physical affection, skin-to-skin contact, being rocked. Those might be some of the things that are applicable for a baby, but for an older child it might be enough stimulation, routine, being listened to, praise, enough structure, opportunities to socialise, being taken regularly to school, being presented in a way that allows you to integrate with your peer group, seeing adults treat each other with respect, being able to learn to negotiate, being rewarded for good behaviour, being treated as an individual and being allowed to gradually develop autonomy.

✦ Each group comes up with lists and we then write each item onto a 'brick' of coloured paper (normally a quarter of an A4 sheet). We use these to make a brick wall on the floor of the room with each of these different experiences building up to help the child have healthy development. Groups often think of 50 or more bricks, and when you make a brick wall of all of those things, what you get is what makes 'good enough' care. You can arrange it, so for example the bottom row of bricks shows the experiences and resources you should have had at 0–6 months and then 6–12 months and then your second year of life, and then your third year, your fourth year and so forth, much like Doodle 5, earlier this chapter. The result is shown in Photograph 1.

✴ We then consider what is written on each brick compared to the child's real lived experience. Did you have enough healthy food? Would someone have smiled at you? Did you get praise? Was there a routine? For each brick, we remove it if the experience/item was absent. If there wasn't enough of the experience/item we tear half the brick off. If there was a skewed version of the experience/item we turn the brick over. Photograph 2 shows the typical results of this exercise – that many or even most of the bricks are missing or skewed, and the wall doesn't look very strong or safe at all.

If a child is placed with a new family, a foster or an adoptive family when they are five, the temptation might be to try and build on the layers of bricks relating to a typically developing six-year-old. Now that would be all very well if all the bricks below it were in place, but unfortunately many of the children with whom we work have missed out on a lot of those basic and essential experiences. For example, maybe they didn't get enough eye contact, they missed out on smiles, they have missed out on routine, they have missed out on a healthy diet, they have missed out on being praised, nobody wanted to listen to what they had to say, they have missed out on having safety. Often when

PHOTOGRAPH 1

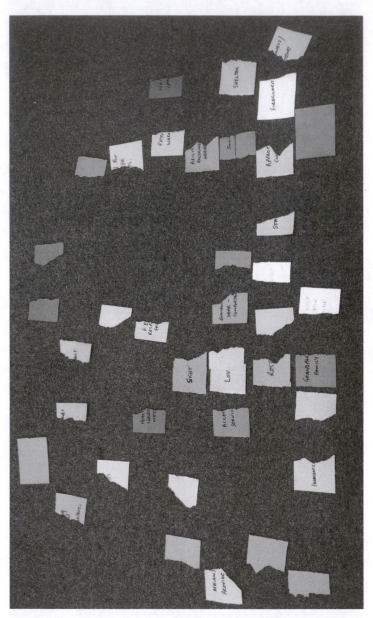

Photograph 2

it comes to children who have been removed from their birth families into Care, there are so many different bricks missing from that brick wall that it is a very wobbly wall indeed. So building upwards is not possible until you have filled the gaps in what is there already.

I think children are amazing because where there are lots of missed experiences they will actively seek out the experiences that will fill those gaps. So children who want to be spoon fed, who want to drink from a bottle, who want to come sit on your lap, who play very immaturely, are doing so to fill a gap in early missed experiences. Once that gap is filled they no longer have the motivation to seek that missed experience and they move on to more mature things. To try and build more mature behaviour without filling those gaps is building a fragile façade rather than repairing what came before it. Although there may be pressure from school and your social circle to try and get the child to be more age appropriate, this might require skills that are not yet learnt, so it can be more helpful to start at the bottom and work upwards, with attunement and empathy taking a priority over academic skills and shaping present behaviour. Quite often it is really helpful to follow the child's lead and let them have times in their day or in their week where they can act in a more immature way if that is what they need. We sometimes call this 'nurture time'.

CASE EXAMPLE: Re-growth

I worked with a boy of about seven when I was training in clinical psychology. His name was Robert and he had been through some really difficult experiences in his early life where his parents were drug users and he was profoundly neglected. When he was in foster care he asked the foster carer whether he could have a baby doll. He would carry this baby doll around and he called it Bobby. He wanted to see how the foster carer would react if *he dropped Bobby. He wanted to play feeding Bobby and putting Bobby to bed and looking after Bobby and re-creating the experiences he had missed in childhood through this baby doll. After six or eight months he asked the foster carer if for Christmas he could have a boy doll that could go in a pushchair. He called that one Robbie and after a few months he grew out of Robbie as well, and was able to be much more age appropriate within the placement.*

I was learning about play therapy at the time and in my sessions he went through a parallel process of wanting to role-play being a baby. In some of the early sessions when we were talking about stressful things, he drank from a baby bottle and wrapped himself in a blanket. I should say I didn't even know there was a baby bottle in that playroom, but he found one and we washed it out so he could suck on it. But just as in the placement, it was simply a phase he was working though. In later sessions he was able to develop more mature behaviour and to start re-enacting experiences with toys and testing out what was okay and not okay about his experiences.

In the group that I run for adoptive and foster parents, making the brick wall is always a really stark visual demonstration of how much is missing from some of these children's lives. Sometimes we build brick walls with 50 bricks and we are left with six or eight bricks when we consider the fostered or adopted children of the parents in the group (see Photograph 2). Sometimes we end up with very small pieces of quite a lot of bricks but no whole bricks at all. It is a strong visual image that lets us realise exactly what the task is of rebuilding those early experiences.

I often encourage foster carers and adoptive parents to really think about what the experiences are that could let the child gain what was necessary from that experience even now they are much older. So if they haven't had the experience of being soothed and rocked as an infant, could they now be taken to play on a see-saw? Could they be tucked into bed at night and have a story read to them, or sit on your lap while you are watching television? Each of those things might repair a missing piece of their early experience.

The other thing to say about the wall activity is that some adoptive and foster parents have tried doing it at home with their child. This works particularly well if the child is a bit older, perhaps of secondary school age. Carers tell me they have replicated the activity and talked with the child about what good care looks like. They have considered what the bricks are that would make up good care at different ages and made the wall with their child, using it as a means to talk about what normal/healthy care is like. Then the child has been able to show what bricks they had or didn't have prior to coming to that placement, which might be the first time they have opened up about some of that information.

Sometimes adoptive and foster parents have been pleasantly surprised by their child wanting to make the wall all over again, this time to look like their current placement, and recognising that there are good things about the care that they are now given. This can be a revelation to the parent because too often adoptive and foster parents think that the child idealises the birth family and does not recognise that anything is better now than it was before. This activity has proven to be a really non-blaming way of exploring differences in care experiences. Certainly some of the foster and adoptive parents I have worked with have been really touched by the experience of their child recognising how much better the care is that they are now getting than the care they received in their birth family or in the sequence of placements before they got to their permanent one. That recognition can be quite therapeutic in itself, as of course the more that you reflect on what was missing and what is good about the new placement, the more chance there is that the child will actively be aware of what 'good enough' care looks like. These are important steps towards gaining attachment security themselves.

The earlier the child has suffered trauma, the more emotionally immature they may be. Helping the child needs to occur at their developmental level. The first task is to build up their trust and feeling of safety in the parent or caregiver. Then the carer can mirror the child's feelings using their face, voice and body language, and use a quiet, simple environment to help them become calm. Eye contact can be introduced very gradually. Intimacy can be very frightening for these children. They have learned to survive by not letting other people get too close, as in their experience this could be dangerous, and by not reflecting on other people's thoughts as this could be too hurtful. Foster carers need to proceed very slowly and gently as fear will provoke these children to withdraw or become aggressive. They need both playful and caring touch as well as other sensory experiences they may not have had. Even children who have been sexually abused need physical contact and cuddles when they request them, or in a gentle and unthreatening way (e.g. putting your hand on their hand when they are distressed). Don't demand kisses or hugs from them; let them choose when they are comfortable enough to offer these.

Children may need to learn about how their bodies feel as they probably had little feedback and help when they were maltreated. They may keep eating when full or need help to know when they are cold or could put on an extra item of clothing. Some bodily sensations like a loud noise or the smell of alcohol can suddenly take them back to traumatic experiences. Recalling these early sensations or traumas can leave children highly anxious and physiologically aroused (ready for fight or flight). They may require 'sensory integration' to help them understand and process sensory stimulation before they can form relationships or talk about their experiences or process their feelings. Children whose world is a confusing mass of sensory information may first need medication, aromatherapy or massage to help them order and regulate their physiological state before they can cope with sensory integration and sensory stimulation.[23] Only then would they be ready to play out or express their experiences or emotions. After that, it may be possible to give words to their feelings and discuss what has happened to them.

---

23   See Bhreathnach (2006) and Hoire (2005).

CHAPTER 4

Shaping Behaviour

I am sure that most of you have watched *Supernanny* or read books about how to manage children's behaviour with consequences. The general message is to reward good behaviour and to punish bad behaviour, so that the child learns to do more of the former and less of the latter. The focus is often on 'time out' or taking away favourite possessions as consequences for unwanted behaviour. The only problem is that these methods rely on the child trusting that the relationship is okay and that they are okay (acceptable as a person) even when they get negative consequences.[24]

Being able to learn from feedback depends on many underlying skills that would allow them to control their behaviour and be motivated to achieve the most positive result. A child who has been abused or neglected or has had a chaotic life might not have a secure sense of themselves as a lovable person who is capable of changing their behaviour and succeeding in life. They may feel that any negative feedback is a threat or indicates impending rejection. They may not trust the security of the relationship enough to tolerate feedback like this. They may feel that praise is not sincere or rewards are not deserved whilst criticism may cut them to the core. They may unwittingly re-create the abuse and neglect they are used to by sabotaging positive

---

24   See Hughes (2006a, 2006b).

outcomes and events, and ensuring they gain negative (but familiar) outcomes.

However, if you've tried the *Supernanny* route and cancelled all the outings, confiscated their PlayStation and favourite toys, then grounded them for a month, it becomes clear that the system isn't working and you are punishing yourself as you are going to end up having to work out what to do with a frustrated child for a month! Consequences only work when the child is able and motivated to achieve the positive outcome. As we've seen with the brick wall exercise, many children who come from a background of trauma, abuse and neglect are missing so many basic experiences that they aren't familiar with the idea of a caregiver who cares about them and holds them in positive regard, let alone one who is consistent about what is expected of them and keen to support them to achieve the best possible outcomes. So they might be suspicious of your motivations for being nice, or so caught up in survival strategies and accumulating the things that make them feel safe that they haven't reached the stage of forming relationships at all. To parent children like that, we have to adjust the balance of behaviour management plans, so that we focus on building the relationship and making clear the expectations before jumping straight to consequences.

More evidence-based parenting programmes emphasise the importance of the underlying relationship and the need to set any behaviour management techniques on top of the solid grounding of an established loving relationship. In the Incredible Years programme,[25] which is the most well researched and long-standing programme for managing children's behaviour, they draw a pyramid of the parenting

25   See Webster-Stratton (2006).

skills that help children to learn best (see Doodle 7). At the bottom they place the most basic skills like empathy, attention and involvement, play, problem solving, listening and talking. On top of this they use praise, encouragement, rewards and celebrations to catch the good bits of the child's behaviour. On top of this they have clear structure, rules and expectations, which are consistently delivered by the parent/caregiver. Then with minor misbehaviour they ignore, redirect or distract. The use of consequences like 'time out' and loss of privileges are the very tiny tip of the pyramid.

This focus on building the underlying relationship and focusing on the positives is even more important with children who have experienced trauma, abuse or neglect. The experience of being valued and held in mind is new to them and really core to changing their way of relating to others, and they may never have had a caregiver who will give them positive attention, or observe or participate in their play, or who will listen to them, talk about their problems and suggest possible solutions. We will come back to the importance of empathy, and strategies for empathising with older children, in later chapters because I believe it is such an important skill. But this chapter is going to focus on attention and play.

✎ Activity: Giving your child your full attention

✦ The challenge is to give your child your full attention for at least 15 minutes, three times per week, on a one-to-one basis. You can work out when to fit it in, and how to occupy everyone else and how to explain it to the child. With younger children you can just say you want to do some fun stuff together. With older children you might need to say you are practising something you read about in a book,

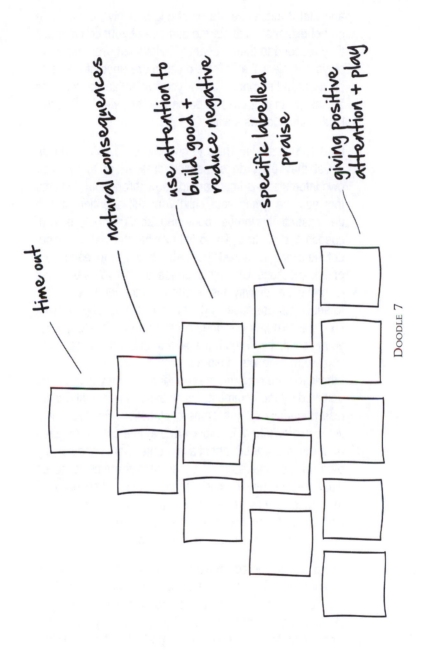

time out

natural consequences

use attention to build good + reduce negative

specific labelled praise

giving positive attention + play

DOODLE 7

and that it might seem a bit strange, or give them some sort of explanation about the purpose of your comments if they respond to them negatively. However, from our role-plays it is clear that it feels much more uncomfortable to do as an adult, particularly if you are unfamiliar with the technique, than it does to be on the receiving end of this kind of attention as a child.

↟ Find 15 minutes in which to give the child your attention whilst they play, do something creative or follow their own interests. It is important to show throughout this time that you are giving your child your full attention and to demonstrate this through body language, facial expression, speech and gesture. Try to follow what the child is doing. Let them lead, do not tell them what to do, try to teach them or ask questions. Only make suggestions if you are invited to, or the play/activity has reached an extended pause. Try to show you are observing them by commenting on what they are doing, or how they seem to be feeling (e.g. for a young child, 'I see you have picked up the green pen, and you are making lots of big round marks with it and smiling. I think you are enjoying making them'). If they seem to be annoyed by the comments, or question them, make them less frequently or give some explanation. For teenagers you could ask them to explain a favourite computer game or music track (or talk about a favourite sport, hobby or any other of their interests). You can take the time to notice what they do, what excites them about it, find out how they do it and pay attention to them discussing their topic. So long as the time is interactive, the same goals can be achieved no matter what the activity chosen.

↟ Establish eye contact, move close, and smile at the child. If you get a chance, use touch as well as words to show you are close by. If you like what they do, pinpoint what it is you like about their behaviour and be specific in your praise. Don't wait for behaviour to be perfect before praising;

praise when it is good for them at that moment. Encourage and praise curiosity, creativity, concentration, patience, persistence, effort.

↳ Don't criticise or structure during your 15 minutes. If the child's behaviour becomes difficult then ignore it if you can, as if you just happened to look out of the window at that moment, but go back to commenting and praising as soon as there is any small shift towards doing something appropriate. If the child's behaviour degenerates to the point that they are aggressive or out of control, just end the session, but aim to build up a longer session next time. If the session has gone well, tell the child how much you enjoyed it and how you are looking forward to spending time with them again. Make sure what you say is sincere!

↳ Playing with your child like this will build the child's confidence and a positive self-image. It helps to develop independent thinking, self-direction, understanding of others and problem-solving skills. It gives a child a feeling of belonging and being valued. It demonstrates that you are interested in their ideas and actions and respect their views, opinions and how they are feeling. It gives reassurance and a feeling of safety, encouraging them to ask for help if required. It helps to develop their listening skills, patience, sharing and negotiating. Play like this also helps develop children's creativity, and social and emotional skills.

NEAR MISSES

In this country, there is a strong culture of telling children what not to do, but it is less common for children to hear what exactly you want them to do. Imagine someone queuing with a child in a bank. It's easy to imagine them being told 'don't touch that', 'don't push', 'leave the pen alone', 'don't do that', 'stop that noise' or any number of negative commands. However, it would probably be more helpful to the child to be told what the parent does want them to do. If a child is told, 'We are going to go in the bank and queue now. It's going to be a bit boring waiting to be seen, so I wonder if you can do some quiet games, like counting things that you can see or seeing how long you can stand on one leg' then that child is more likely to be able to succeed at the challenge than at one they are not prepared for.

CASE EXAMPLE: Learning from feedback

I think back to the process of teaching my husband to drive. I don't think that would have been possible to have done by only telling him what not to do. I'm sure there were one or two moments of 'don't cross the centre line of the road...no, don't go so near the pavement...don't go so fast when you turn' or similar, but the majority of teaching involved preparing what we were going to do and then giving constructive criticism for what had taken place. So, I remember lots of preparation conversations like, 'The next thing we are going to do is practise turning right, so when we leave this parking space, you'll take up your normal road position but get ready to indicate and move the car outward slightly towards the centre of the road so that you end up on the right of our side of the road by the time we reach the give way sign. Do you feel ready to do that?' And when we had undertaken a manoeuvre we would discuss what went well and what could go better next time, like, 'That was much better than before, I felt like you had more road awareness of the key hazards so I wasn't scared this time, but if you wanted to make it even better you could think about slowing down more gradually ahead of known obstacles like roundabouts.' This strategy of preparation, practice and then feedback is also very helpful for children to learn how to behave.

When you tell them what you want them to do, children can visualise themselves doing it. If you tell them what not to do, they cannot visualise what they should do instead. Worse still, they may imagine themselves doing the wrong thing as you describe the 'don't'. If you say, 'When we go to visit your nan, don't touch her china ornaments', then they are only picturing the china ornaments and touching them. It could work better to say, 'When we go to your nan you can play with her stone pebbles and stroke the cat.'

It is also important to make the praise and positive feedback you give both sincere and specific. A generic 'Good boy!' or 'Good girl!' is not as helpful as, 'It was lovely to see you give that pen to James when he asked. I really like it when you share so nicely with your brother.' Similarly, gushing praise for something small might feel false, particularly to a young person who has not had much positive feedback in their life. So, they might allow you to say 'Good effort' in a fairly quiet voice but find it uncomfortable or doubt your sincerity if you say, 'You are so fantastic, that was really excellent!' You will need to watch the reaction closely and draw on your experience of this particular child to pitch the feedback at a level they can tolerate and benefit from.

The other opportunity is to capitalise on 'near misses'. So, if the child tries to act as you've advised or in a more appropriate way than normal, but this does not go well or is not sustained enough, you can seize the opportunity to praise the effort and recognise the change from the past pattern, but then give feedback about how to be even more successful next time. So, for example, saying, 'I can see that you tried to be patient with your sister when she started winding you up, and even walked away like we discussed, that's great. Perhaps next time you can come and get me if she follows you, rather than pushing her over?'

When setting targets and consequences I'd very strongly advocate that a positive focus is the most effective. So, on a sticker chart you must never remove stickers for bad behaviour or have sad face stickers that are chosen instead of smileys if the target is not achieved. Also the rewards must be arranged such that each target can be attained and have a meaningful response, as it must always be worth choosing the positive option. For example, if you are working on sharing, with the day broken into seven slots which could each earn a sticker, and you set the target of five stickers in a day earning a consequence (e.g. ice-cream after dinner), then if the child misses the first three sticker opportunities in the day, for the rest of the day there is no motivation to comply because no reward is possible. If, however, you offer ice-cream in return for five stickers no matter how long they take to earn, then every sticker earned gets you a step closer to your goal. It is also important to set achievable goals and to work on something on which the child is capable of gaining an 'easy win' in a relatively short time, to show that you genuinely intend to follow through on the promises made. This will also give both you and the child hope that change is possible.

A favourite technique of mine is to print a picture of something the child wants onto a sheet of stickers, and let them gradually assemble the full picture sticker by sticker as a consequence of good behaviour to earn the reward. The picture might be of a new football, or the local park (to earn a visit there), or pancakes, a book or game they want, or the computer (to earn time on it).

When praising your child, remember their emotional level as you may need to exaggerate the positives as you would for a much younger child. Or you may need to start with very gentle praise and positive experiences so that they are not too overwhelming. Similarly, handling separations needs reassurance with clear demonstrations of joy at reunion as with a much younger child. Remember that children most need to be loved when they seem most unlovable!

Another helpful thing to remember is that disagreements tend to become an argument where each side ups the ante as they go back and forth, with each desiring to assert control over the other or 'win the argument'. A small comment you make to the child might get a snappy response, which might lead you to tell them off, which might lead them to have a tantrum, which might lead you to feel like you need to impose a sanction, which might make them more angry. Each side is trying to win at the cost of the other, and success or compromise becomes more and more unlikely. Where it is possible, it is a really helpful strategy to diffuse anger by acknowledging the other person's perspective and any legitimate aspect to their grievance. So, for example, 'I know it's really frustrating to turn off the telly, but we need to go' is less likely to lead to a negative outcome than, 'Turn off the telly, we need to go, otherwise you'll make us late again.'

The other alternative is to opt out of the argument and to choose to do something else entirely or to give an unexpectedly positive consequence, as this can be a different way to win the battle. For example, if a child is repeatedly difficult in the week leading up to a particular treat or positive experience there are many parents who would feel that in order to assert some discipline the child should not be allowed to go. However, many of these children have practised being punished and neglected and missing out on nice experiences many times in their lives, but have rarely had the opportunity to experience being rewarded and having positive experiences. So, it might be more helpful to comment that the child seems to be acting in a way that leads to punishment, but that it's time to change the pattern and go and do something different instead (e.g. an energetic activity, a soothing activity, a snack).

For example, it might be that the idea of going to a party or on a holiday is so threatening and feels so undeserved that a child appears to want to sabotage their opportunity to participate by being repeatedly challenging. The parent either continues the pattern of disappointment and rejection or has the opportunity to say to the child, 'You know what, even though it's been a really difficult week and I think the idea is making you a bit anxious, I think it would be a great experience for you to learn how to have more fun, so we are going to go anyway.' Some people worry that this is 'rewarding misbehaviour', a sign of weakness or backing down and feel it is important to 'win' to assert control over the child. However, your ability to choose the outcome the child does not intend or expect is the real show of being the one in control!

Even within discipline you can offer your child choices to give them some control. 'You can carry on shouting and we will leave the shop without buying any shoes or you can be quieter and we will buy shoes – you decide.' Make your rules for behaviour and your expectations very clear, spell out the consequences for broken rules and be consistent.

CHAPTER 5

Effects of Parenting on the Infant's Brain

When a baby or toddler is exposed to something frightening or threatening, their internal systems prepare them to protect their safety by using 'fight, flight or freeze' where they would run away if they are mobile or become silent and still if this is not possible. (The fight part is more prevalent when the child gets older and has the ability to fight back.) If there is continued harm the infant or child might mentally escape by learning to take their concentration away from the physical sensations that are happening to their body. As adults we have similar instincts for fight or flight (but normally will only use 'freeze' or mentally escape through dissociation if this is something we have learned as a child).

These responses effectively allow us to escape or defend ourselves when there is danger and are an excellent survival mechanism. They involve the body sending out chemical messengers called cortisol and adrenalin which make lots of changes to the pattern of activity in the body and the brain. In the body, the message prioritises blood-flow to the muscles, and slows down the digestive system (after encouraging us to quickly empty any waste we are carrying). We become more active and restless, and notice signs of the changed blood-flow like sweaty palms, churning stomach and a dry mouth.

In the brain, the amygdala (an almond-shaped bit on the bottom of the horseshoe-shaped section in the primitive central part of the brain) becomes very active, and the prefrontal areas (where we do our most sophisticated thinking, like empathy and understanding cause-and-effect) become much less active. I have shown where these areas are in Doodle 8. This change in brain activity is very helpful because at times where our safety is at risk, we need to prioritise survival even where that means not being too sophisticated or logical. That is why you hear stories of people who have done incredible things 'in the heat of the moment' like lifted huge weights or withstood huge forces to protect their child, because under these extreme stresses the logical part of the brain that would say 'I can't do that' is much less dominant than the part which urges fight or flight, even when this would cause damage to the body or isn't in our long-term best interests.

Doodle 8

When an infant is distressed (whether through fear or anger or discomfort), their body and brain go into this fight or flight mode, until the perceived danger abates. However, they are not very good at differentiating different feelings yet, and in distinguishing what is a genuine threat, so that is something they need to learn from the adults around them. One of the things I have found very interesting has always been how intuitively most parents help children learn to regulate their levels of physiological arousal (readiness for fight or flight). If you have a baby that is crying, as a parent you will intuitively jiggle and stroke the baby, then slow the pace of the jiggle or stroke down and then bring the baby to your body so that it has lots of skin contact and is cuddled in safe and warm against your body. If you have a toddler who is having a tantrum, as a parent you will normally acknowledge that with quite a loud voice and large gestures, noting what has caused the distress. You would then pick them up and you make patting and/or jiggling motions and gradually slow it down as you bring the volume of your voice down to offer some soothing comments and tell them it will be all right as you cradle them in to your body. All of that is very intuitive, so much so that you might never have noticed it.

What most people don't know, when we are doing that, is that we are matching the high level of arousal, the fast heart beat, the fast breathing rate with the volume and rhythm of our movements and as we slow it down we are modelling that it is okay for the heart rate and breathing rate of the infant to slow down. We are demonstrating non-verbally that the level of physiological arousal they are experiencing is not needed for fight or flight and does not need to remain so high. When we bring a child to our body, the skin-to-skin contact releases oxytocin, a very calming, loving chemical that is involved in a pre-programmed soothing system which overrides cortisol and quietens down the amygdala and lets the child regulate their arousal to a lower level of readiness for fight or flight. When we hold the child so that their head is on our chest or shoulder (which are the most common positions for a cuddle), we are letting the child hear that our heart rate and our breathing rate are not in a highly physiologically aroused state. This allows the child's heart rate and breathing rate to slow down to match. Such co-regulation is instinctive because at a survival level the body is primed to match the arousal level of other people around you. When cuddled against the parent's body, the infant realises at this primitive level that the adult has a greater awareness of potential danger and that the adult does not feel it is necessary to be so physiologically aroused. They are then able to calm themselves to match.

By doing those intuitive things (being attuned to the child and helping them when they are in a state of distress to calm and to regulate) we are teaching children how to activate their soothing systems and moderate their level of physiological arousal. Infants who have this experience of a containing adult learn to gradually recognise and manage their own feelings effectively. Careful research on infant development has shown that you need to learn to co-regulate before you can self-regulate. If a child has not experienced an adult who is able to regulate their level of arousal, and to help the child to do likewise, then that child is unable to do anything with their fight or flight state except to fight or run until the neurochemical messengers run out. No effort of reasoning or consequence will help them to do otherwise, so the key to helping them to learn self-regulation skills is for their carers to model self-regulation and to help the child to recognise, calm and control their emotional states.

NEUROPSYCHOLOGICAL DEVELOPMENT

We know that babies experience the world at a sensory level, without pattern or meaning. The world seems initially chaotic but they then start forming patterns and recognising some of the sensory information to be a consistent parent figure. They can then begin to attribute meaning to different experiences. This allows the infant to start developing much more sophisticated functions in the brain, particularly those located in the prefrontal areas of the brain. For example, they are able to see events as having a sequence with a beginning, middle and end. They learn that things have cause-and-effect relationships. In time we come to understand what the impact is of our behaviour on other people and what the consequences are likely to be of different choices.

Some of that is the beginning of empathy and the beginning of having a sense that other people experience the world in a way that is similar to us. We start to recognise the difference between thoughts and reality. We begin to label emotions and understand what causes them. We gradually understand that the mental process happens for other people in a similar way to us but they might not have exactly the same thoughts and feelings. Research has shown that a good nurturing and attuned parent helps to develop those skills of cause-and-effect reasoning, and empathy and self-monitoring, and theory of mind in an infant, so children who have been through very deprived or chaotic parenting experiences and early life experiences often have difficulties in those areas. Patricia Crittenden[26] suggests that the avoidant child develops their thinking and sacrifices their emotions, and the anxious ambivalent child develops their emotions and sacrifices their thinking.

Creating coherence and meaning is a really important process and is normally one that happens very early in a child's life and is accompanied by structural changes in the brain. When a baby is first born, a lot of neurones are in place but they do not have many connections to the other neurones around them. Over the course of the first two years of life, it is the connections that grow massively in number and help the brain to start linking up ideas, and thinking and making much more sense of the world. It is through increasing interaction with the world, having some consistent responses and having consistent people that the child gradually learns to make sense of it. This search for meaning, achieved through this proliferation of neural connections in the first two years of life, is a really important factor that differentiates the human brain from that of any other species. There are even researchers who jokingly say a human baby is born two years premature, because those connections that are not in place yet at birth for movement, for sensory recognition and for language are all learnt during those first two years.

After the first two years the connections within the brain that are not used are pruned back. Over the following eight years until the child is about ten more connections do grow, but it is harder to repair later the experiences that should have led to connections being formed before the age of two and the brain was optimally plastic (in the sense of being able to change and develop). After around the age

---

26   Avoidant and anxious strategies with emotions and thinking. See Crittenden
      (1997).

of ten when the second round of pruning happens in the brain it becomes extremely hard to make up for missed experiences, so extended periods of deprivation really have quite a catastrophic effect on the brain. We know from cases of children who have survived in really adverse circumstances or have been profoundly neglected and abused that a child who has not been exposed to enough human language before the age of ten rarely develops full language skills. The more profound the absence of experiences is in those first years of life, the harder those deficits are to compensate for later on.[27]

However, research shows that when it comes to early intervention, it is quite an encouraging picture. If you change a child's life experiences before they are two, they can make remarkable change and recovery. In the years between two and ten they can make significant recovery, and certainly the studies of maltreated orphans in the Eastern European orphanages left by the Ceausescu regime have shown amazing progress, even if there is not usually a total recovery.[28] The effect on the brain is really profound from severe neglect. One thing I have learnt over the last ten years is that the earlier you start to compensate for missed experiences the better. We also know that the earlier maltreatment happened, the more impact it has on the brain.

When we think about young children who have been exposed to poor care, the changes are not just at a structural level (in the brain), but affect how the children function and how they feel. Maltreated children also learn to have different beliefs about themselves, the world and others. (These are the core beliefs or schemas that underlie our

---

27   Impact of early deprivation. See Uylings (2006).
28   See Roy, Butter and Pickles (2004).

way of thinking.) If you have had a secure caregiver who has given you attention and positive feedback, and has enjoyed your company and been stimulating and playful with you, then you learn that you are an okay person, that other people in the world are likely to be okay to you and that the nature of the world and your experiences is likely to be benign and safe. If you have had traumatic abusive early experiences then you learn to believe that you are not okay as a person, that there might be something bad or flawed about you, that others will generally treat you badly and are not to be trusted, and that the world is a very dangerous and scary place. Those underlying beliefs profoundly impact on the child's self-image, their expectations of relationships and the way they treat others. Interestingly, the beliefs about the self, others and the world formed by not having a secure carer are the type of beliefs and schemas that underlie anxiety and depression and other mental health conditions in adulthood, if they remain unchallenged.

CHAPTER 6

Through the Generations

A parent is also your first model of relationships, and the resource that equips a child for life. I like to think about it using the image of balloons,[29] which are shown in Doodle 9. If you imagine a parent as a balloon, their job is to inflate the baby balloon with enough air to float into the world of good relationships and to be able to cope with the challenges and knocks of life. An effective attuned parent is able to use their own resources to fill the balloon, and to protect it and help it become independent, by tying a knot to hold in the air. The parent is 'internalised' by the child, who can draw on their skills and experience to become an on-board puncture repair kit in times of stress. The child balloon can continue to inflate itself internally and through other healthy relationships, and is both resilient and able to float up to where other healthy balloons are, where it can form relationships. If a parent does not have many emotional resources, then their balloon is not effectively filled and it will struggle to fill up the child. They might see the child as a potential source of air, rather than recognising how much of their own air will be required to inflate it. Or they might remain mouth-to-mouth with the infant balloon as they do not know how to separate or provide the tying off

---

29 With thanks to colleagues from Action for Children in Scunthorpe who introduced me to this metaphor for Object Relations during a workshop on building self-esteem in 1999.

that will keep the air inside. The baby balloon is unable to internalise that 'puncture repair kit' and therefore easily punctures under stress. So without another balloon constantly inflating it, the balloon easily sinks to the ground amongst other punctured balloons and the risks of many prickly obstacles.

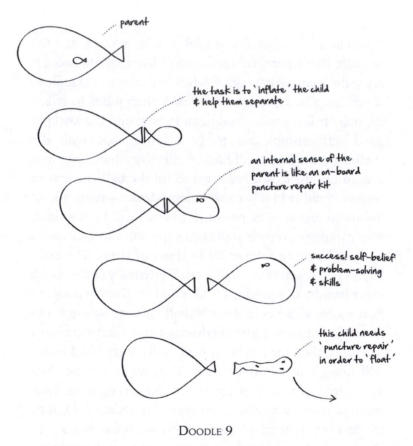

DOODLE 9

Many carers tell me how exhausting it is to constantly try to inflate a 'leaky balloon' of a child and how it takes up all their own air. So my task as a therapist has always been to attempt to help parents (with additional tools and knowledge, and perhaps some of my own air at times) to inflate and tie off the balloon of their child, or to complete puncture repairs, or to work with young people or adults to repair their own puncture wounds and create their own puncture repair kit, to enable them to float higher in their future lives and relationships.

Doodle 10 illustrates how patterns of attachment transmit through the generations. This is something we have already touched on, and it might be self-evident from the balloon doodle that a parent with limited emotional resources is not always well-equipped to set up their child with those emotional resources. However, I think it is worth mapping it out a bit more and then thinking about how adoption and fostering (or other changes of placement) affect things.

As I hope you will have gathered by now, you need a certain level of internal security to hold your child in mind (that is, to constantly consider their experiences and feelings) and create that kind of predictable and nurturing life experience for a child to develop optimally and have a secure attachment. So if you have a parent who is able to hold the child in mind, they can then teach the infant to recognise and regulate their emotions, to have empathy, and to have good social and negotiating skills. That infant will be able to connect with more socially appropriate peers. In my metaphor they 'play the tea and cake game'. They will learn all the positive social skills that will help them be successful in life (we call these pro-social skills).

If you picture a nursery, there is often a kitchen corner where well-adjusted children very often will play games of making people food and drinks. If one starts playing then other children will recognise that game and know how to join in. So if you put a set of three- or four-year-olds

parent who can
provide a safe base

↓

attuned parent
holds child in mind

↓

child learns :
empathy
theory of mind
social skills
self-regulate

↓

child gains a template of
healthy
relationships

↓

they choose partners who
could offer empathy & stability
they think seriously
about when & how to parent

have a child of their own

Doodle 10

together they often play at making each other cake, or making each other tea, or cooking other familiar food for each other. When offered play food by another child they will say, 'Oh what a lovely drink of tea, thank you very much' and they will have that kind of very over-learnt social hospitality embedded in their play. A child who has learnt all of those good pro-social skills will make friends with others who have those good pro-social skills. Whereas if in that nursery there was a child who had been exposed to a very different kind of lifestyle, they might not know how to play those tea and cake games, because that might not have been the lifestyle they experienced or something that was taught to them.

Let's imagine the play of a child who has been brought up in a house where they were profoundly neglected by parents who misused alcohol. A child in those circumstances might re-enact their life in the home corner in a very different way. They might even sit down on a chair and slouch back and say, 'Oi bitch, bring me a beer.' Now if someone else in that room has had a lifestyle like that they might know how to play that game, they might know how to interact to play out the experiences that they have had in their family circumstances. So children with similar experiences are drawn together. And when you have got children as young as three or four who are already socially grouping according to the kind of parenting experiences they have had, it is no surprise that people go on to form their later relationships with people with similar attachment experiences, because just as the children have common play, they have common language.

This is reinforced by the fact that if you come from a very high emotion household where you have had to be ready for fight or flight at all times, the very well-behaved children will seem boring and dull whereas the children who are getting into lots of trouble will be a match for your level of physiological arousal. Children like this will have very sensitive threat systems within their brain, but very under-developed soothing systems.[30] This means that they seek out excitement and conflict and activity; they are neurochemically matched to all that adrenalin that goes with the excitement. So people group for a number of reasons with people who have similar background experiences.

Reflection: Spotting patterns

Have a think about your own social network. How similar are your friends' attachment patterns to your own? Maybe they have been through different life experiences, but are their beliefs about parenting and the nature of their relationships similar? We often associate with people with similar attachment patterns to ourselves, and pass on our own experiences through the generations. Many parents report being surprised to hear their parent's voice coming out their own mouths to their children, or otherwise re-enacting experiences that they had long forgotten.

For example, it might be that most of your friends are in long-term relationships that are successful, and where there is divorce and separation it is handled in a fairly amicable way. Or it might be that most of your friends chop and change relationships and have lots of fights and fallings out with each other.

These clusters of similar patterns also pass on from parent to child. I think about that in terms of the patterns that pass from one generation to another (which we call transgenerational cycles). What happens is that a parent who holds the child in mind and offers secure and attuned care

---

30   Neuroscience of trauma: threat systems and soothing systems. See
     Cozolino (2002).

creates a healthy pattern for the child (see Doodle 10). They are able to protect the child from harm and soothe them when they are distressed. This high quality care teaches the infant how to recognise their feelings, to regulate and soothe them when they become physiologically aroused, to link cause and effect, to read others with effective empathy – important components of social skills. The carer reflects how much they enjoy and value the baby, so that the child learns that they are valuable and lovable. They gain their identity and self-image within the positive mirror of the carer's experience of them. They learn that other people are reliable and sensitive and that the world is mostly safe and benevolent. The child then learns the building blocks of how to form healthy relationships and as that child gets older some of those healthy relationships go on to be romantic relationships. A young person with insight about the importance and demands of parenting then tends to take quite seriously the prospect of having a child themselves, so they plan (as best they can) the time at which they would want to have a child. They would typically decide to do that within the context of a healthy relationship or with a good support network around them, and so when they become a parent they have the capacity to hold that child in mind and the cycle can repeat itself.

If I were then to draw the cycle of what happens in a child where the parent does not have the capacity to hold them in mind, the picture would be quite different (see Doodle 11). Here the parent is chaotic, perhaps unavailable or unpredictable or even harmful at times. This means that the child is placed in a situation where their innate threat system is triggered. To compound this, they are not soothed sufficiently, and the parent does not teach them to regulate their arousal. The parent is in 'survival mode' where they

neglectful / abusive / chaotic
parent

↓

can't hold child in mind
(too busy surviving)

↓

child does not learn
empathy
theory of mind
social skills
self regulate

↓

child gains dysfunctional
template of relationships

↓

is attracted to exciting
but chaotic relationships
& lifestyle

↓

they may hope baby
will fill gap or have
unplanned pregnancy
in chaotic circumstances

have a child of their own

DOODLE 11

don't have the emotional capacity to consider the baby's experience beyond providing basic care, and even that might vary according to other stressors such as domestic violence, their mental health or substance misuse. So the infant does not learn those skills about empathy and to link cause and effect; they just learn from the mirror of their carer that they are a bad child and deserve maltreatment. The infant gains poor self-image and beliefs that others and the world are dangerous, critical or unreliable.

The developing infant does not gain those social skills that the child in the previous family learnt. They are primed for threat and maintain quite high arousal. This child goes on to be the child who takes risks and may be more aggressive, or they might be withdrawn and aloof. They may play the games that are very exciting or dramatic and get involved in conflict, for example through bullying or being bullied. They may play the beer game instead of the tea and cake game and form exciting but dysfunctional relationships. They are more willing to take risks and experiment with drugs and alcohol. As the child becomes an adult and those dysfunctional relationships become sexual, they often become pregnant in an unplanned way. This means that a baby might arrive to a teenage parent, and/or without much planning and in the context of relationships that are not very healthy, characterised by parental conflict and/or substance misuse. They may go on to parent that child without appropriate support or in a dysfunctional relationship, and the baby experiences a parent who is in a chaotic state and repeats that cycle.

PATTERNS THROUGH THE GENERATIONS

It is worth thinking about the patterns that we ourselves come from and those that our children have experienced.

It is not always as polarised as these two extremes, but it might be that traits you thought were passed down because of it 'being in the genes' or because of some kind of organic disorder the child was born with could in fact be the product of their parenting experience. The study of epigenetics is beginning to shed light on these differentiations. We will come back in a later chapter to considering the superficial similarities between children who have been exposed to poor early care and have damaged attachment templates with some common diagnoses.

Reading about the patterns that transmit through generations and the fact that attachment patterns can stay entrenched for a long time or be changed in a positive direction by a change of placement, you might be wondering about change in the opposite direction. What about people who are in a good pattern but then end up going through so many stressors that they move onto a more negative track, for example due to a destructive relationship? The first thing to say is that having had a sound footing in secure attachment relationships is very powerful – children who get good care in their first couple of years tend to make quicker recoveries and do better overall even when they experience abuse, neglect and chaotic care than those who lack that initial foundation. In the same way, one secure attachment relationship, even if it is not with a primary carer, can also provide resilience in this way. It is also worth saying that attachment styles are quite stable, and it takes a fairly major event or accumulation of events to significantly change how a person's attachment style functions.

However, there are some people who go on to be a parent and then face lots and lots of stresses which will inevitably impact on their parenting (e.g. if they live in a war zone, or have a very destructive relationship, or they are seriously injured or unwell or have a mental health breakdown). Hopefully, securely attached adults form healthy relationships with others who are securely attached and so choose good partners and a supportive network, but our life experiences can change. For example, you can go into a relationship that becomes progressively worse until it becomes so destructive that you become less and less secure. Having had a secure attachment helps people to recognise the shortcomings of such a relationship and the need to protect the children, but life is not as simple as that, and children are sometimes exposed to stresses even by parents who had good childhoods themselves.

However, if those parents have had the background experiences of being parented effectively then a lot of their intuitive responses are probably still protective even though their lifestyle is chaotic due to factors outside of their control. Plus they are more likely to have good sources of social support to prop them up under stress. The experience of having a parent who is temporarily under stress generally turns out to be less damaging for the children than if they have come from a background in which they have become accustomed to incredibly chaotic situations and simply don't recognise the risk or the harm that is being done. But of course this varies from situation to situation and person to person, because there are so many different variables at play.

The interesting thing about trauma is that there is a dose effect.[31] The more you are exposed to trauma, the more people who are involved in that trauma or perpetrating harm, and the longer you are exposed to it, the more impact it has on the child. Normally, stressors that a parent with a healthy template will be dealing with

---

31   See Reed *et al.* (2005).

tend to have a much milder impact on the child than a chronic pattern of dysfunction which is repeated through a sequence of similar dysfunctional relationships, or due to chronic substance misuse, or being passed around a family. Similarly, we know that children do better when they are removed earlier and reach permanence (a family placement intended to last until adulthood, such as adoption or long-term fostering) without too many changes of placement in the interim.

It is a sad indictment of the current lack of placement choices and training/support for foster carers that we are not always able to provide such a pathway, and that children may be removed and rehabilitated back to the birth family several times before being permanently removed, or go through a series of short-term placements before finding their 'forever family'. Even then, not every placement runs smoothly and there appears to be a lack of accessible and skilled support when problems begin to appear.

There is also a major problem at the moment in achieving permanence for children aged over seven because of the lack of long-term placements available. Sadly, because of the lack of choice, the placements are not always matched ideally to the child, and some carers are encouraged (either financially or due to the demand for placements) to take on more children rather than being able to focus on just one. And of course every placement that comes to an unplanned ending worsens the prognosis of the child.

CHAPTER 7

Changing Patterns
The Tug of War of Attachment

Whilst we are considering what happens across the generations, one thing which is interesting to think about for social workers and adoptive and foster parents is the fact that sometimes we are trying to remove a child from the unhealthy transgenerational pattern into the healthy transgenerational pattern (see Doodle 12). What is often very difficult to know with a real-life family that you are involved with is when you should intervene, unless there is a single terrible incident that becomes a catalyst for intervention. However, to me it really highlights the importance of decisive early action, because if you remove that child very early they can learn empathy, self-regulation and pro-social skills, and may be able to go on and form healthy relationships themselves. If you leave it too late then the child may have already developed some quite entrenched patterns of forming dysfunctional relationships and that work becomes harder.

Some people suggest that this means the main focus of intervention and the deadline for adoption should be in relation to babies and infants under two years of age. However, although these children do the best when placed into alternative families, there is good evidence that children under five generally thrive in new homes, and that the majority of children placed with high quality carers and appropriate professional support can still be successful

neglectful / abusive / chaotic parent
↓
can't hold child in mind (too busy surviving)
↓
child does not learn empathy, theory of mind, social skills, self regulate
↓
child gains dysfunctional template of relationships
↓
is attracted to exciting but chaotic relationships & lifestyle
↓
they may hope baby will fill gap or have unplanned pregnancy in chaotic circumstances

have a child of their own

parent who can provide a safe base
↓
attuned parent holds child in mind
↓
child learns: empathy, theory of mind, social skills, self regulate
↓
child gains a template of healthy relationships
↓
they choose partners who could offer empathy & stability, they think seriously about when & how to parent

have a child of their own

DOODLE 12

in permanent new homes even when they are six or seven or eight years old. Permanence is successfully achieved with certain types of children and certain types of carer even into adolescence. So in my view aiming for permanent placement within a family wherever possible is still worthwhile, because even if the change does not happen fully within one generation, there are still improvements in that child's quality of life, and intervention can also make positive impacts on the next generation. That is because those children then go on to be more likely to become earned secure and to offer more attachment security for their children than they would have been if they had stayed in the very chaotic life within their birth family.

Professor Marinus van IJzendoorn did an analysis of all the studies[32] of the outcomes of adoption. He describes adoption as being the most powerful intervention ever studied, describing it as more effective at changing the long-term results for children than aspirin is at reducing pain. His research shows us that the outcomes of children adopted early enough change from those of the deprived, abusive and chaotic pathways in which they were born to being the same outcome as would statistically be expected of the birth children of adoptive families. They gain in all kinds of outcomes including IQ.

I believe the outcomes are so remarkable because adoption takes children out of chaotic socially deprived families and puts them into families that are very committed to the acts of parenting – those who have chosen to do parenting for a living in the case of foster care, or who have desperately wanted a child and have thought about it a great deal in the case of adoptive parents. This means that the people who

---

32   This process of compiling all the data from multiple studies is called a
     meta-analysis.

adopt or offer other forms of permanence to children are generally the people who can hold a child in mind and they tend to be in less chaotic, slightly better socio-economic circumstances with less stressors than the birth families.

Van IJzendoorn's studies show us that adoption works brilliantly before the child is two and the data tells us that you can be pretty optimistic about adoption before the child is five. But sadly, the older the child goes beyond five, the more risk there is that the patterns are entrenched and that the placement will not last them until adulthood. By the time the child is nine, around half of all placements break down. One of the tasks of professionals is to recognise the need to intervene decisively and intervene early, because that can mean a difference of a generation in how fast we change these patterns. However, the data is incomplete at the moment because there are limited studies following up children who are adopted later which explore the factors that are related to risk and resilience, and the impact of providing the right packages of support for those whose placements are the most risky because of the age and experiences of the child.

DOODLE 13

I find it helpful to think about what happens to a child's attachment style in a placement and the impact they have on the people around them with the image of a tug of war (see Doodle 13). Whether children change their attachment pattern or not is about the balance between competing forces: the parents trying to make the child more secure, and the child trying to make everyone else less secure (though the latter is not a conscious or deliberate process). Typically the tug of war happens when a child who is from an insecure attachment pattern gets placed into a new family who are not used to that pattern.

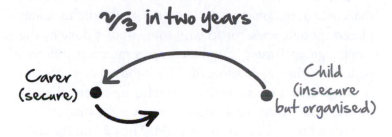

DOODLE 14

Let's assume for the sake of Doodle 14 that the child is placed with a family who are in the secure category and let's first consider what happens if they have a child placed in their family who is one of the organised but insecure categories. What happens in that scenario is that there is a tug of war in attachment styles: the child's behaviour and way of behaving and relating to others encourages the carers to become less secure, and the carers' way of behaving and relating encourages the child to be more secure. Each of them is familiar with the patterns that happen in their own backgrounds and behaves according to their own patterns learnt from their own life, and finds the other's patterns a bit disconcerting and unfamiliar. Perhaps the child perceives the household as too quiet, and is only used to calm periods as short intervals that precede a storm, so they learn to provoke the storm to get it over and done with and to burn off that fight or flight chemistry they are used to producing in their body and brain. The parents, on the other hand, are used to a nice quiet life and experience the child as constantly misbehaving and provoking needless conflict. We'll come back to patterns of physiological arousal (readiness for fight or flight) in the next chapter.

But let's think about that tug of war a little more in the context of some of the research that tells us about placement outcomes, particularly some studies done by the Coram group[33] using play-based assessments at different periods of time after adoption. If a child who is insecure but organised is placed with carers who are secure, the pull on the carers is to make them react in ways that are less secure and more familiar to the child. The pull on the child is that these carers are doing things differently, that they are reacting in a way that creates a secure base and gives the child the opportunity to learn that way of behaving. If the carers can stay in that secure position (which is something that we will come back to) then the research tells us that two thirds of the time in a two-year period they win that tug of war and the child becomes secure. That is an amazing outcome and shows the power of living within a new family. I find the Coram group follow-up studies quite encouraging in terms of who wins that tug of war.

If you have a child who is insecure disorganised, it is as if they are a step further away from that secure pattern that you need to create, so the tug of war that happens is more intense (see Doodle 15). These children make a much stronger pull on the carer to disorganise and become less

---

33   Changes in attachment style in permanent placement. See Kaniuk, Steele and
      Hodges (2004).

secure and that puts pressure on the carers' relationships and on the placement, which is more at risk of breaking down. However, if the carer can remain secure, that child will gradually become more organised in their attachment style. The research suggests that two thirds of the time in a two-year period they will reach a position of being organised insecure (the middle attachment category and point in the diagram) and they are just as likely over the following two years to continue to go on to become secure.

DOODLE 15

That is a fairly optimistic diagram but it does beg the question of what happens to the one third of children who get stuck in their disorganised pattern (at the far right of the diagram) and the one third who get stuck in the organised insecure position (in the middle of the diagram). Well, I think two things happen. One is that despite their best intentions the new parents do not always provide a secure base and are not always able to sustain that. Although adoptive parents and foster carers are selected because of their ability to provide a healthy attachment relationship and good quality of care, I know that it is not always the case that they are in the optimal secure category themselves at all times. This is particularly the case with adoptive parents, who have often been through a lot of quite traumatic experiences in their own life and have had stressful experiences of fertility treatment or lost pregnancies or relationship breakdowns. For a significant proportion of adopters, the very fact of having to accept an adoption as a means to have a child, rather than a birth child, is a huge psychological challenge. There is then a long, stressful process of being approved, and there may often be compromises from their image of a newborn baby to the reality of adopting a child from the Care system with a complex history. Whatever the story that has led them to adoption, the process often contains pressures that bring them out of the secure category themselves or make them more vulnerable to the challenges that the children bring.

There is a different but equally interesting pattern that applies to foster carers, who have often chosen to be carers as a career and have had to make compromises and sacrifices with their lifestyle and the impact of foster children on their birth children and relationships. They may have children they care about moved on to other placements or rehabilitated back to a birth family (even where this may not appear to the carer to be in the child's best interest), or they may require a certain number of children in placement to make ends meet. The amount of support available is variable, and so are the needs of the different children who are placed. Foster carers themselves, interestingly enough, are quite often in the 'earned secure' category because they have often been shaped by childhood experiences that are not ideal, but because they have become very resilient they are motivated to pass on some of that resilience to the children who are placed with them.

As a result of these multiple stressors at play in the parents, the attachment patterns the children bring can seem to amplify small manageable sources of stress into bigger issues. Some placements break down, some couples split up. In some placements, the stress brings out unhelpful patterns in the parent which they didn't know existed or thought were resolved. Sometimes carers see themselves behaving in ways that they are not very comfortable with, and start to doubt their ability to parent. When that happens they are not able to sustain their secure patterns as a way of looking after that child. That is one of things that we will come back to in 'Patterns That Suck Us In' (Chapter 18), because it is really important to maintain those healthy patterns against the child's disorganised pull in the tug of war. This might involve using what I call your tag team, the people who can take over from you and give you a break or support (as in team wrestling) when you are getting sucked in.

When considering why it is that some children get stuck and parents do not always win the tug of war, part of the difficulty is that sometimes carers themselves are unable to maintain a secure base. I also think that part of the difficulty can be that when you place sibling groups together, they can reinforce the familiar level of emotional volume and attachment style between themselves, so that it becomes harder for carers to change the children's behaviour. I acknowledge that there are big advantages in keeping siblings together for other reasons, like their identity and to avoid any further loss of attachment figures, and understand why this is considered positively by social services and the legal system. However, I think that when you place large sibling groups together you need to be a little wary, especially if you believe the children involved have an insecure disorganised attachment style. In my experience, the larger the group of siblings, the stronger the pull is towards maintaining their attachment style and the slower the journey is to moving towards the adoptive or foster carers' attachment style, and the higher the risk of placement breakdown or long-term difficulties within the placement.

However, even when parents are able to make a secure base, there are some children who are stuck in the disorganised insecure category and seem to resist the pull towards organising their attachment pattern. In my experience those young people get stuck there either because they are so dysregulated in terms of their arousal (their emotions are out of control) that they are unable to be in a state where the right parts of their brain are active, or they resist the kind of nurture that would help them to change. These children can also be so aloof that parents find it hard to build a relationship with them, or they are so chaotic that it becomes extremely hard to be an active and nurturing parent, and the placement is at much greater risk of breaking down. This is more likely to be the case if they have experienced very severe or very early trauma.

When children get stuck and don't seem to be organising their attachment pattern at all within the first 12 months in placement, I would really think about requesting specialist input from local services. This might include getting a referral to the local Child and Mental Health Service (CAMHS) team, where a psychiatrist could consider whether medication would be a helpful part of that package, and maybe a clinical psychologist or specialist therapist could consider the type of therapy that would support the family further. Getting help at the right time is critical, because I think if you are stuck in the disorganised category and that pattern is not changing, it becomes increasingly risky over time that the placement will not be sustained. Placement disruptions (a polite term for placements which end in an unplanned way) are really damaging both for the children and for the adults who care about them and have tried to offer them a home. Preventing placement breakdown in the high-risk groups is where services need to target most support.

Another thing that is worth commenting about when considering the tug of war of attachment is just how important self-care and getting the right support is for foster and adoptive carers. This is essential, because it is your support network and your professional network who can help anchor you in that secure position. If you are feeling like you are in it alone and that this tug of war is dragging you in, you really need to bolster up that support network, because it is not a job that one person (or even a couple) can do in isolation.

I believe very strongly that we should be recruiting a wide variety of adopters and foster carers. This should include single people, couples and other family configurations (e.g. an adult alongside their parent/s) and should include people from different socio-economic groups, ethnicities, lifestyles, genders, sexualities and ages. In fact I believe all a child needs is one or more people who will love them, value them as an individual and put their needs first. However, to effectively do this more demanding version of parenting (which is in itself the most challenging job most people will ever undertake) and remain healthy and resilient with sense of humour intact, that person (or people) will need a considerable support network to draw on. Neither adoption nor fostering is a one wo/man job, so you need to think about where you get that support from. This is more essential the further to the right in that diagram the child is when they are placed with you, because actually the more people who are around with positive secure attachment styles, the more modelling of that the child experiences. But also the carer is reinforced in their own healthy patterns and is less likely to be sucked into the unhealthy patterns that the child has brought with them from their past.

This book, and the groups I run, are all about feeling skilled and supported in the challenge of parenting children who have experienced poor early care, trauma, neglect and/or abuse, to increase the chance that placements have a positive outcome. This information and support is intended to maximise the impact that the parent or carer can have on the child's attachment template.

ACTIVELY CHALLENGING YOUR CHILD'S ATTACHMENT TEMPLATE

Part of making the best impact in re-parenting your child comes from recognising and actively challenging your child's unhealthy learnt attachment patterns. Research following up the Coram study that I referred to earlier shows that when foster and adoptive carers are more aware of their child's attachment pattern, and challenge it more overtly, the child's attachment pattern changes more quickly towards a more secure pattern. Thus it is very helpful if you are able to recognise the pattern your child is showing, and then apply particular techniques:

- Avoidant children, whose parents have become anxious or rejecting when they made emotional demands, learn to exclude their own dependency needs and become self-sufficient and emotionally self-contained. Displays of need or vulnerability in others or dependency feelings in themselves can make them feel anxious and avoidant. The challenge for their carers is to help them to access and understand their feelings, especially those involving dependency and vulnerability.

- Ambivalent children whose parents were insensitive have learned to increase their demands and show distress to gain a response. They are desperately worried about being ignored or left alone and not having their needs met. They appear angry, dissatisfied or provocative in relationships, but also ignore their own thoughts or behaviour. The challenge for carers is to help them feel loved and valued but also to understand their own relationships and behaviour, and to be content enough to tolerate separation.

- Disorganised children do not know how to react as their parents have been the source of their fears and abuse while also being at times their supposed source of care and support. It is very difficult for children to regulate their emotions when faced with unpredictable danger and inconsistent care. They have confused expectations of relationships and may only feel safe when they are in control of others, and their feelings and needs are denied. The challenge for their parents or carers is even greater: to help them to feel safe with a caregiver and to acknowledge their own feelings. It will take time for them to realise that they can be loved without also being abused.

When children have suffered unpredictable and frightening situations, they feel helpless and anxious when they are not in control. They particularly need consistency. When they feel vulnerable they can become hostile or withdrawn. The child may cope by becoming very self-reliant or desperate to please or cutting themselves off from their feelings, but all of these make it harder to form a meaningful relationship with the child. It is best for foster carers to consciously resist being drawn into the avoidant, self-reliant and controlling dynamics of the maltreated child. The challenge for the foster carers is to remain nurturing even when children give out a message that they do not want care and support.[34]

---

34   See Dozier *et al.* (2002).

CHAPTER 8

Arousal Revisited

I want to think a little bit more about arousal levels (the body's level of physiological readiness for fight or flight) because I have touched on it but haven't really explained it fully. I hope it will be helpful to come back to all of the different aspects of what a child learns from a parent who can hold them in mind, because those are really important in terms of how that child develops and their mental health. Later I'll be considering how these issues relate to particular diagnostic labels that might be considered with some children, such as autism spectrum conditions (ASC) or attention deficit hyperactivity disorder (ADHD).

From my conversations with adoptive and foster parents, and also with social workers and education staff, it seems that despite the importance I feel it has in my understanding of looked after and adopted children, arousal level is something that hasn't received enough attention.

As I have mentioned already, basically what happens is that our life experiences (including the time in the womb) tell our body how ready for fight or flight we need to be. Children who have been exposed to violence produce more cortisol and are more primed for fight or flight. They are sensitised to look for threat signals because the amygdala in the brain is more active and the frontal lobes less so. There is less empathy and ability to reason and more tendency to see situations and other people as a threat, and they tend to have poorer attention and concentration and be more impulsive, resulting in more behaviour problems. The worst combination in terms of neurological development is to have exposure to violence without the affection and nurture that triggers the release of oxytocin, a feel-good neurochemical I mentioned earlier that is related to closeness, empathy and love that infants release when cuddled or given skin-to-skin contact.

I've tried to draw what happens in your brain and body in terms of physiological arousal (readiness for fight or flight) in Doodle 16.

DOODLE 16

If you live in calm and safe circumstances, your body might have become used to being at level one on a scale of 1–10 ready for fight or flight. So, you might be going along through your life at one out of ten on a scale of physiological arousal (like the lower line on the chart) and then something stressful might happen: someone might get into an argument with you, someone may drive inconsiderately, you might have to go through an interview experience, and your stress level and your readiness for fight or flight will go up. Your body will release adrenalin and cortisol and it will prime the muscles to get ready to run away. Your blood-flow will prioritise a different pattern in your body, where energy is transported to your muscles as opposed to your digestive system. Similarly, different parts of your brain get more or less active according to the amount of adrenalin and cortisol that is around.

On the scale we are using you might raise two or three points for a particular stressor, or even four or five points with a major source of threat or anxiety. It makes that little hill on the chart. You stay in that state just for a short period of time and usually, as the danger passes or after about half an hour to an hour, your level of arousal comes down again and you go back to your normal level. Because you have not reached very high on this scale of arousal your brain is still quite active and analytical; the frontal parts of your brain that you use for empathy, to self-monitor, and to judge cause and effect are still very active, so you can be reasoned with at any point in that process and you can apply logic and learning.

However, if your life experiences have taught you that it is necessary to have a baseline of five out of ten readiness for fight or flight because there is a lot of chaos and conflict and trauma and raised voices about, then you might look more like the upper line in the chart. If those same levels of stresses come along (you get into an argument, someone drives inconsiderately), and you rise the same two or three points on the scale, the results are different. That peak in your arousal level takes you above a threshold at which you go into a kind of survival mode. Something happens within brain activity that means that the amygdala (which is the fight or flight sensor in the brain) becomes extremely active. Like a car alarm going off in your brain, it overrides everything else, and the frontal parts of the brain become much less active so your priority becomes just to survive.

When that happens we are left relying on older parts of the brain, and we go back to very primitive ways of behaving in order to survive. So we fight, we run away, we freeze. We don't think logically, we don't do analysis, we don't do empathy, we don't think through the consequences of our behaviour. Now that's really helpful as a survival skill, because if you are attacked by a bear you need to be able to run. If you are attacked by a snake you may need to fight it off. If your child gets stuck under a rock you don't need logic telling you, 'Oh, I probably can't lift that and I don't want to damage my muscles.' You want that surge of adrenalin and blood-flow to your muscles that makes you able to lift that rock and move it, no matter what the cost is to your personal health and physical integrity.

So it is a really helpful response in context. But if you break that threshold in a conflict in your family home or school, then there is a peak during which your level of arousal is so high that it is very hard for you to be reasoned with, or to apply any empathy or learnt skills at all, because you are in survival mode. At those points you have to just wait until the adrenalin and cortisol has been burnt off or gone down or do something to soothe the person. If you remember, the soothing system and its chemical messenger oxytocin are the way to trump the messages of cortisol and adrenalin and the activity of the threat system to bring that arousal level down. If you are trying to soothe a child who is in that survival mode, the most helpful calming things you can do are at a non-verbal level, because appealing to reason isn't going to help whilst the appropriate parts of the brain are not active.

It is also worth noting that whilst a person is in a state of high arousal they tend to interpret neutral signals as being threatening, so even quite benign situations can keep that arousal level high, such as the noise and movement in their classroom at school, or any raised tone of voice or sudden noises. They might assume that jokes or partly heard conversations are about them, or see facial expressions of concern as being critical.

EMOTIONAL VOLUME

Sometimes it might seem that there is a total mismatch between the level of arousal of the child and the level of arousal in your family, and that the child is constantly drawing you into a state of higher conflict and tension than you would like. If you think about the 'emotional volume' that is happening in a household, it is almost like imagining the car radio. If you have come from a very chaotic household, that car radio has been set very loud and it might not fit in with the volume in the adoptive or foster home. If you imagine driving in your car during the course of the day, you might start out at your house turning the radio on when you start the car. Then you might drive on the motorway and turn the volume up a little because of the traffic noise, then there might be a rain storm or even hail, and you might be stuck in traffic and wanting to hear the news, so you might turn the radio up a bit more. When you park the car for the evening, the radio might still be on the louder setting. When you get up in the morning and go back to the car and turn the engine on, the radio is suddenly too loud because you are not in an environment with enough background noise to merit that level of volume.

I tend to think that the children who are placed in secure households have a higher set level of volume of emotion or conflict than is required by that environment. So they are trying to turn the volume up because that is more familiar and the parents or carers are trying to turn the volume down. The image of seeking a familiar emotional volume is another way of thinking about this tug of war that is happening at so many levels between the child's attachment pattern and that of their new family.

Arousal is quite contagious – when you see someone else rise in their readiness for fight or flight, our own level of physiological arousal intuitively rises to match.[35] I find that fascinating, but it makes a lot of sense in survival terms to be alert to threats perceived by others. What happens is that the more you are around people who are dysregulated (highly emotional, and in a state of increased readiness for fight or flight) the more likely you are to dysregulate yourself. So if somebody starts yelling at me, it is very hard physiologically for me to stay calm and not to get ready for fight or flight myself, and if I get ready for fight or flight myself then physiologically it becomes more likely that I perpetuate their conflict by shouting back at them. However, just as arousal is quite contagious, so is soothing. This means that if we are calm then others with us are also calmed by that. When with others who are calm, we are more able to feel relaxed and at ease, particularly when we have soothing sensations or are in skin-to-skin contact with others. You will remember that this is the work of the chemical oxytocin, which is associated with love, sex and nurture.

If we are able to remain calm as adults, we can soothe children and they can feel calmed by it, but when someone

---

35   Contagious effect of arousal. See Nummenmaa *et al.* (2012).

dysregulates (e.g. becomes extremely angry or fearful) it instinctively dysregulates us. So it is really important when you are parenting that you don't let the child's behaviour lead you to dysregulate so much that you can't help the child to regulate. This means that when you feel that the child's behaviour is causing you to rise in physiological arousal (signalled by feeling tense, shouting, or being physically rougher or more agitated) you really need to use your tag team. If you feel yourself getting angry or having bodily sensations associated with an increase in physiological arousal (such as sweating, clammy palms, churning stomach, dry mouth, sense of tension or restlessness in the body) this is when you should use your support network and get someone else to come in and support you in calming down the child, and support you in calming down yourself. It is a really good skill to model that you know when you are beginning to dysregulate and you take time out. Dysregulation doesn't have to lead to conflict.

We also know that children need to learn to co-regulate before they can self-regulate, so if they haven't had that experience of being soothed and cuddled and stroked then they will find it very hard to bring down their own physiological arousal levels. They will often create or enact some kind of conflict or physical activity until that chemical is burnt out. It is really helpful for those children if we can find a way to help soothe their level of physiological arousal. However, when they are a bit older, it becomes more difficult to pick them up, jiggle them, pat them, stroke them and bring them to your chest as you would a younger child. But ideally you would still do broadly similar things. You would go and sit with them, you would talk in quite an animated loud way to match their level of arousal to acknowledge their distress, and then you would gradually start talking more calmly. When it feels safe to do so, you would make some physical contact. Ideally you would pat them with a rhythm and you would then slow that down and turn it into a stroke, and wherever possible you would end up with a physical cuddle that involves skin-to-skin contact and a position where they can hear your heart rate and your breathing rate.

Once the child is soothed (and the frontal area of the brain is back on-line), you can start to explain things to them, or appeal to reason and past learning. You might be able to help them connect the story of what has happened into a logical sequence, explaining how they might be feeling. It is good at this point to be aware of the child's shame – the sense that they are a bad child who is unlovable and deserves to be maltreated – and we will return in a later chapter to considering how we can respond to that in an empathic way. Routine can be helpful and soothing to highly aroused children. Have the same routine each day (or one for school days and one for other days) and warn children in advance about any expected changes to it.

It is also helpful to be aware of the fact that many of their past patterns might be playing out, and their responses might have been learnt ways of coping with damaging experiences. Often behaviour communicates what a child can't say in words. I tend to think of the image of an explorer, like Indiana Jones, hacking his way through the jungle towards the temple where he thinks the treasure is hidden. He follows his compass and hacks away a path through the thick foliage with his machete. This takes a lot of effort, because it is cutting a new path, but it is going in exactly the right direction. However, if some threat appears, like an angry tribe with spears or a predatory animal, he would run where there is already a path. In the same way it takes traumatised children real effort and energy and dedication to learn new behaviour patterns, and under stress they will behave in old familiar ways, no matter how inappropriate they are or what the consequences will be. The more stress there is, the more cortisol is released and the less the child is able to reason and access learnt behaviours.

However, when a child is in a calm, soothed state they can begin to use and develop their prefrontal cortex, the most sophisticated and 'human' part of the brain. This area lets us think about thoughts and feelings, the past and the future, and the impact of our behaviour on ourselves and others. It lets us have empathy for other people's experiences and understand that their minds operate in a similar way to our own, although they will have their own goals and preferences, due to having different life experiences. That understanding of the nature of minds is known as 'theory of mind' and is an important building block in social skills. It is the beginning of the reflective capacity that allows us to change how we behave and to challenge our existing patterns (important if we want to form different types of relationships).

Interestingly, recent research suggests that the prefrontal cortex continues to develop throughout childhood and is only completely functional from our early twenties. So, this is an area where we continue to develop more and more sophisticated skills for a prolonged period of time, and where our experiences and relationships continue to influence our development long beyond the development of the connection patterns in other parts of the brain. However, it requires a rich and stimulating environment, and enough calm and safety for these pathways to develop.

I used to think that whether you were in a state of calm or a state of threat was a simple two-sided game of trumps in the brain, according to whether the cortisol or oxytocin was dominant, but recently I have been learning about a third system that is at play in the brain that makes me think it might be more like a game of paper, scissors, stone. This third system involves the chemical messenger dopamine and is associated with activity, excitement and the acquisition of status and possessions; in short, anything we find rewarding. It is dopamine that is involved in addiction to any activity and this 'drive' is why we often turn to action when we are distressed, or collect things (or go shopping) in the hope that it will make us happy when we are unable to self-soothe. This is why when attachment doesn't work well and the child doesn't learn to soothe themselves and regulate their physiological arousal, this can increase the risk of dysfunctional patterns in later life, even if it does not show in the form of aggression or anxiety (fight or flight). Again, this will be something we come back to in later chapters.

CHAPTER 9

The Calm and the Storm

I talked in the last chapter about the pattern of arousal and how this can lead to outbursts or conflict. We also know that these 'blow outs' can be quite reinforcing, by creating the high emotional volume that is familiar to the child and reinforces their perceived sense of threat because they trigger a negative response from those around them. Sometimes when a child or an adult comes out of that patch and they've burnt off a lot of adrenalin and cortisol, there can be a little dip after the big peak on the chart in which they are more able to contact feelings that are vulnerable and empathic and tolerate feeling warm and close to people. This means that the aftermath of a blow out is sometimes found to be very rewarding by the person and those around them, who value the feelings of being close to people after the conflict. That's a tricky situation because you don't want the aftermath of conflict to be the only time at which you can access the child's warm feelings, otherwise it reinforces the need to go through this conflict cycle.

As I have previously mentioned, people who are accustomed to very high levels of fight or flight readiness (very high levels of physiological arousal) feel a bit disconcerted in environments that are too quiet and calm because it feels like 'the calm before the storm' and the longer that they are in calm the more disconcerted they feel, until they create the conflict that allows them to discharge the adrenalin and the cortisol. Obviously that doesn't happen at a conscious level, but parents often tell me about how it takes smaller and smaller triggers to tip the child into an outburst when they've been having a prolonged length of calm, because of the adrenalin and cortisol building up. It is also useful to remember that adrenalin is also the messenger involved in excitement, and thus it is very easy for the physiological arousal that accompanies pleasantly exciting events (such as treats or celebrations, particularly if these are unfamiliar) to switch the child into fight or flight.

The other thing to say about conflict is that we have learnt from domestic violence situations[36] that if there is a woman who has previously been a victim of domestic violence and the man comes home in a state where she is picking up cues that there might be violence, she will not always act to prevent this. Although it might seem counter-intuitive, even if he is giving signals of impending conflict, the woman does not always choose to escape the scene or do everything in her power to avoid the conflict. What she does in many cases is that she provokes the conflict. This may not be a conscious process, but it allows her to have more control, to get it over and done with more quickly and to get to the reward in that dip afterwards where he is saying sorry and telling her he loves her and it will never happen again, when they are feeling close and are having a closer sense of attachment. Obviously I'm not suggesting that anyone is consciously thinking, 'I'd really like him to

36 When explaining this concept I am using the example of the gender roles which are most commonly reported in domestic violence cases recorded and I am not meaning to imply that domestic violence is exclusively perpetrated by men against women. I am well aware that there are perpetrators of both genders, and that domestic violence occurs in same-sex relationships and between many different configurations of family members (e.g. between adult siblings, or between parents and their adult children) and similar patterns would apply. However, for simplicity I have used the pronouns related to the majority gender configuration.

hit me now', but there is some kind of skewed learnt logic that says that if I am in that kind of situation I might as well get it over and done with and I might as well get to the good bit faster.

Similarly a lot of children who have been through traumatic experiences also have that same pattern where if they sense a parent, carer or another person is becoming at all annoyed or threatening (or when it is too calm), they provoke an incident to burn off the conflict as quickly as possible. It makes a great deal of sense as a survival strategy based on their skewed past experience, and they may also have been rewarded by a time of closeness from their parent afterwards. If this is the only way they have experienced affection or nurture then they may also provoke an incident when they feel like they need more containment and more affection and more closeness because that it is their way of getting there.

CASE EXAMPLE: Blacking out

I have worked with several young people where their experiences have been vividly described to me as going beyond a rational threshold and losing conscious control of their behaviour. For example, there was a teenage boy who had been through some really pretty extreme violence at the hands of his parents (including being beaten with a dog chain) and who had been referred to CAMHS because of episodes in which he in turn had been very violent towards others. When I asked him about those incidents he would say, 'Something winds me up and then I black out. When I come to I find out what I have done.' He would talk about 'coming to' having smashed windows or having caused other people injuries or with bruises or blood on his body and not knowing consciously what had been going on, and he found that experience very scary.

People around him were sceptical about his apparent 'split personality'. However, I think he was a very extreme example of what happens when the amygdala is so active that the logical, rational, reasonable part of the brain (the frontal area) is not active. Sometimes children learn to cope with extreme experiences of violence by blotting them out of awareness and this can become a habit, as soon as extreme fear or anger is present.

If anger is as extreme as this particular young man described it, then it sometimes really helps to have a medication that can help bring down their arousal so that their baseline is one or two points lower on the chart and they have a higher capacity before going through that threshold at which they lose cognitive functioning. This would be something worth discussing with CAMHS, particularly if there are aggressive episodes or very frequent conflict and normal consequences are not having an impact.

The effects of trauma, as I have mentioned, are dependent on dose and timing. We know that the arousal chemicals of adrenalin and cortisol travel through the placenta and if the mother is being exposed to a great deal of domestic violence or conflict or a chaotic life then those chemicals will be travelling through the placenta to warn the baby that life is very dangerous and they need to be primed for fight or flight. Because heightened arousal levels are so tied in with our survival instincts, they are remarkably persistent over time. I've certainly met children of four or five or six who still have a raised baseline level of physiological arousal because of exposure to trauma when they were in utero (as most of the key neurochemicals pass through the placenta from the mother to the foetus) or as a very young pre-verbal infant. Some of the most extreme examples of elevated physiological arousal that I have worked with have been people whose mothers experienced chaos and trauma during the pregnancy and who were again exposed to trauma or domestic violence in their very early part of life, which confirmed the necessity of that raised arousal level. Once established, those arousal levels take a long time to change, even in a calmer home. We know that when children witness or experience violence prior to the age of one (and that includes in the womb), it has a profound effect.[37] Children who were exposed to domestic

---

37   Impact of very early exposure to violence. See Carpenter and Stacks (2009) and O'Connor *et al.* (2002).

violence during this period still play more aggressively with neutral toys at age six and eight.

Reflection: Readiness for fight or flight

Have a think about your own life. Have you felt the impact of threat, stress or anxiety at any point? How did it feel in your body? How much control did you have over it? Where are you now on the scale?

How about your child? Did she/he have reason to feel under threat or stress at any point (including whilst in the womb)? Where is she/he now on the scale? Does anything cause that to increase or decrease?

It might be worth testing out whether regular exercise or relaxation can influence your child's level of arousal. Exercise would need to be vigorous and sustained enough to burn off the neurochemicals that are having a negative effect, and relaxation would need to be regularly practised and supplemented with relaxing activities. Certain repetitive physical activities can serve both functions, and I have met many families where the trampoline has proved to be an essential piece of kit for this reason. The materials provided by Relax Kids (www.relaxkids.com) can be useful when it comes to teaching the child to soothe their body and brain, as they include some lovely CDs of relaxation exercises on varied child-friendly themes such as magic, nature and space.

It might also be useful to see whether providing feedback to your child by commenting on their state of arousal, and noting times that might potentially be stressful to them (such as long periods of calm), can help them to pre-empt dysregulating. Therapy techniques such as Theraplay, a method of using playful activities to compensate for missed nurture experiences and improve the attachment relationship, can also build on this.

CHAPTER 10

Diagnoses

I have discussed in earlier chapters how the attuned care of a secure caregiver teaches a child to self-regulate, have a positive self-image and learn the building blocks of empathy and social skills. Where these are absent it can end up looking like certain developmental disorders (see Doodle 17). As I have detailed, exposure to chronic trauma during development leads a child to have a heightened readiness for fight or flight and to emotionally dysregulate more easily. As I explained in the previous two chapters, we know that the increased presence of cortisol and adrenalin has a profound effect on the body and brain. We know that raised levels of arousal are associated with changes in blood-flow in the body, with increased blood supply to the muscles and less to the organs and digestive system. There are also changes to which sections of the brain are more active, with more activity in the primitive brain and less in the sophisticated prefrontal areas.

These changes in blood-flow and brain activity show in the child's behaviour as difficulties with concentrating, higher levels of motor activity, being more impulsive, having less ability to see the consequences of actions, difficulty reading social cues and an increased tendency towards aggression. All of those look like what is now known as Attention Deficit Hyperactivity Disorder (ADHD), which may be subdivided into 'inattentive' and 'hyperactive' subtypes, or called the more British name of 'hyperkinetic disorder'. Although trauma-based hyper-arousal might look superficially like ADHD, biochemically it is hypothesised to be from a very different cause.[38] ADHD is hypothesised to be a lack of activity in the frontal areas for neurochemical reasons whilst traumatic hyperarousal is caused by overactivity in the amygdala leading to shut-down of the frontal areas. ADHD is therefore often treated with stimulant medications that increase that frontal activity, whereas chronic exposure to trauma might need a different form of treatment, as there is already a heightened level of arousal in the brain.[39]

hyper - arousal   (ready for fight or flight)

— difficulties with attention
— restlessness
— hypervigilance (to everything !)   **? ADHD** like
— quick to turn into anger
— difficulties with self-regulating

difficulties with social skills

— avoid reading other people
— lack of empathy   **? ASC** like
— poor social learning
_ needs structure and predictabilty to cope

DOODLE 17

---

38   However, the research to date has not identified a simple difference in brain chemistry or anatomy or a single genetic carrier for ADHD, suggesting that it might be a combination of different factors.
39   Brain activity in children who have experienced trauma. See Teicher *et al.* (2003).

Other diagnostic labels that might overlap with the presenting features of exposure to trauma and poor experiences of attachment include those on the autistic spectrum. This is a cluster of conditions where the brain is not set up to process information in the same way as in the majority of people. The typical results are difficulties with social understanding, difficulties with flexibility of thinking, and difficulties with the social aspects of communication. This means that people with autism might struggle to make friends, to behave in a socially appropriate way or to cope with unpredictable variations to their routine, and might not be able to adapt their communication to the audience (typically monologuing on topics they are particularly interested in, without reference to the response of the person they are talking to). They have a poor understanding of emotions and the feelings of others.

Autistic behaviours are often associated with the tendency to need a lot of order and structure (e.g. lining up toys or being very precise about time, or becoming anxious or unable to cope when plans change), differences in response to sensory information (e.g. reduced reaction to pain, enjoyment of patterns and lights, highly sensitive hearing) and increased rates of learning difficulties and disabilities, tics, fits, attention difficulties, language problems, dyspraxia (lack of motor coordination, often including clumsiness) and other developmental difficulties. People with autism also have a tendency to become preoccupied with narrow interests, to collect factual data and to be confused by subtle expressions of emotion. They often struggle to adapt to different circumstances or to understand what is expected of them unless it is explained in a very specific and concrete way.

Autism is a spectrum of different presentations, which range from quite a subtle pattern to one that is profoundly disabling. The extent to which autism impairs functioning is also affected by the level of ability the person has (generally it is much more disabling when combined with learning disability), the nature of any other difficulties they have (e.g. ADHD, epilepsy, dyspraxia, language disorder, Tourette's syndrome) and the amount of support and structure that is available to them. Sometimes the milder presentations or those where the person is highly intelligent are given the diagnostic name of Asperger Syndrome or high functioning autism, or they might be given a label of autistic spectrum disorder (ASD) or autism spectrum condition (ASC) as the diagnostic labels vary between individuals and over time. I will use the acronym ASC to refer to presentations on this spectrum.

If a person has ASC, the extent of their difficulties may appear different at different times in their life. The amount of problems they experience and the amount to which their behaviour is atypical or would be viewed as noticeably odd to others varies according to their development or the amount of stress they are experiencing. Some people can appear to be profoundly autistic in their early childhood, but their presentation can become more and more subtle as they develop and learn compensatory skills, such that they can function very well as an adult (see Temple Grandin's autobiographical works[40] for example). Others can appear more able but regress or show more unusual behaviour when under stress, or where there is significant change or uncertainty (e.g. when changing school, or when on holiday).

---

40   Grandin (2006, 2008) and Grandin and Scariano (2005).

People with ASC seem to see the world in a more logical and mechanised way, and struggle to understand the nature of people who have thoughts and feelings that are not visible and might act in ways that are not always rational and predictable. There has been a lot of research exploring the nature of this difference (which appears to be at least partly a genetic trait) and trying to localise differences in the brain, though the exact mechanism is still a mystery. However, it is clear that people with autism have a less intuitive sense of how other people think and feel. We call this 'theory of mind': having a working model of the nature of subjective experience.

Research indicates that to gain an effective theory of mind you need both the biological capacity inbuilt in the brain (which, it is hypothesised, people with ASC lack) and the early experiences of being held in mind by another, normally your parent or carer. This process of someone constantly considering what you think or feel and reflecting your emotions back to you allows you to learn to recognise and name your emotions, to learn to regulate them, to experience empathy, and to learn to use the frontal parts of your brain to be aware of your own thoughts and feelings and those of others (which may be absent for people with early abuse and neglect). You will see from the above descriptions that there can be considerable overlap between the presentations of people with ASC and those who have experienced poor early care and abuse.

For example, there are many academic papers published about the 'quasi-autistic' presentations of children removed from the highly deprived orphanages of Eastern Europe.[41] When the adopted Romanian orphans were four years old, many showed a pattern of difficulties indistinguishable

---

41   See Rutter *et al.* (2007).

from autism. By six years some were showing more flexibility in communication and a more social approach, but sometimes indiscriminate friendliness. After their adoption many had developed circumscribed and repetitive interests. At 11 years, the researchers followed up all the adoptees with social communication problems and did a thorough assessment and diagnosis. One in nine of the adoptees showed the quasi-autistic pattern, but they were more likely to lose some of these features as they grew older than children in the general population with ASC.

As these very extreme examples of deprivation show, it seems that severe neglect or chronic poor care can lead children to present in a very similar way to autism. The nature of the brain, which remains highly plastic for much of early childhood, means that it is often difficult to distinguish the source of any impairment. However, there are some distinguishing features that I've been exploring in my research.[42] Possibly the most obvious differentiating factor between ASC children and those who have experienced abuse and neglect is how the child relates to adults. Children with ASC tend to relate to them just like any other object in their environment and not pay them too much attention, whilst many children who have experienced abuse and poor early care are very vigilant towards adults, even if they don't respond to them in the same ways as children who have experienced 'good enough' care. Children with ASC also tend to be blithely oblivious to teasing or social rejection from their peers, whilst those

---

42   It seems that people with ASC and those who have experienced abuse and neglect both have poor theory of mind and struggle to understand other people's thoughts and feelings. However, children with ASC seem to give more incorrect explanations as to why other people use non-literal language than those with poor early experiences, who are more likely to express confusion or give a physical explanation instead.

who have experienced abuse or neglect are very sensitive to signs of rejection and may even interpret neutral cues negatively (e.g. seeing a concentrating facial expression as one that is cross with them). However, there is still a need for more research about the outcomes for the two different groups.

It is also worth acknowledging that a lot of children who are in the looked after system might also have organic difficulties as well as having experienced social adversity. Children in the looked after and adopted system have higher proportions of certain kinds of conditions than in the general population. This would include a range of developmental disorders like ASC and ADHD, learning disability and mental health conditions. The reason for this is twofold. Firstly, parents with these kinds of traits are more likely to have difficulties with providing 'good enough' care for their child and therefore are more at risk of having their child removed into Care. Secondly, children with these kinds of traits are more challenging to parent effectively and are likely to show more profound impairments more obviously when given deficient care.[43] It may be that a parent can just about cope with meeting the needs of a developmentally typical child, but struggles to meet the needs of a child with a developmental disorder. Of course, it may also be that profound neglect and exposure to poor care can actually cause the child to appear developmentally disturbed.

This is a complicated subject for professionals to consider because there is a tendency to assume that if you see certain symptoms that are diagnostic of a biological

---

43   Looked after children are more likely to have developmental disorders, or
      mental health problems. See Ford *et al.* (2007) and Howard, Kumar and
      Thornicroft (2001).

condition or if a child has been through abuse or neglect, that becomes an explanatory factor for everything they are presenting. Probably the wisest path is somewhere in between the two: to acknowledge that there are often combinations of organic and acquired difficulties. Such combinations are often bigger than the sum of their parts, in the sense that the combination of a disorder like ASC or ADHD or learning disability with adverse experiences like having been abused or neglected can create incredibly challenging presentations, much more so than would one of these conditions alone.

CASE EXAMPLE: I don't understand the risk

I was asked to assess a 15-year-old young lady called Lindsey on the children's ward after an episode of deliberate self-harm. She had taken an overdose of cough medicine, and it was the 19th time she had been known to A&E since moving into the area two years before. Each time she had called an ambulance for similar reasons, such as having drunk shampoo, or eaten unidentified berries, or taken tablets. When I went to assess her, I was able to read her health and social care notes, and neither contained any record of any underlying condition. However, both made reference to how she had experienced abuse and neglect, and then multiple changes of placement, and was 'a very troubled young woman'. I felt that she had difficulty understanding which substances she was consuming genuinely posed a risk to her health. She was unable to understand that taking eight co-codamol tablets might be very dangerous to her health or even fatal, whilst 20 vitamins or cough sweets might pose less risk.

When I completed a cognitive assessment and explored her level of social understanding and theory of mind, I found that Lindsey had a Moderate Learning Disability (her IQ was in the bottom one child per thousand, meaning that her understanding would have been more typical of a child of under four years of age). She also had very poor theory of mind, obsessions about the route that her foster carers drove to different locations (including the numbers on the lamp-posts that they passed, and whether the cat was sat on the right wall) and a number of narrow rigid interests suggesting autistic traits. The underlying developmental disorder, despite it being really quite serious, had been overlooked because of what was known about her history.

We were able to work with her carers and the local ambulance crews and A&E staff to ensure that she had a very boring experience of being taken to hospital and waiting for blood tests, and was sent home to await the test results without being admitted to the children's ward unless medical treatment was necessary. We also added numerous nurturing activities that would be offered when she had not self-harmed for a few days, such as doing face-packs, hair styling, nail polish or hand massage with her carer. Most importantly, the level of autonomy that was expected of Lindsey was reduced to a developmentally appropriate level, and greater support was offered in education, which reduced her levels of stress. Over the following month the incidents of self-harm reduced, and she had only one ambulance call-out in the following year.

If you suspect that your child also has an organic disorder, professionals may need to help you map that child's development over time to differentiate the two, and it may be that combinations of strategies will need to be tested out, including those that are relevant to particular conditions as well as those that are relevant to traumatised and neglected children. However, as a general rule of thumb, the interventions that are helpful for children on the autistic spectrum or with ADHD are helpful and not harmful for children who have attachment difficulty and whose symptoms are there because of exposure to trauma or neglect. Similarly, the strategies that are helpful to children who are traumatised or neglected are helpful rather than harmful to children who have neurodevelopmental disorders.

One of these strategies that is useful for both groups of children is to always remember that they have a limited understanding of the social world and of how other people think or feel. Whenever you are discussing an incident with them, always include the social information they may not know. For example, they might be hit by another child and think they are being bullied, because they do not always understand their part in the build-up to what the other child did. They may not be able to differentiate what is accidental and what is deliberate, or to understand other people's motivations. For example, you may need to explain that the other child did not like it when they pushed them off the trampoline, that other children like to share, and that the trampoline belongs to all the children. It was not right for that child to hit them, but it was also not right to push them off the trampoline. Similarly, it is not enough to tell them not to grab items from others, without explaining that other children don't like it when things they are playing with get taken, and that each person should have a turn with an item and that other children will not like to play with them if they grab items when it is not their turn.

CHAPTER 11

Understanding Thoughts, Feelings and Behaviours

Clinical psychologists don't work to a medical model in which symptoms are seen to represent underlying disease that can be diagnosed and treated with medication. We like to look at a wide range of biological, social and psychological factors that combine to make a particular presentation, often grouping these into predisposing factors, underlying beliefs, triggers and maintaining cycles, and look at how these lead to challenging behaviour, emotional distress or difficulties in relating to others. We call this process 'formulation' and it is used to try to understand what has led up to a behaviour, what influences it, and what interventions might help it to change.

Don't worry if you have not heard the word before. Formulation is not a frequently used concept, despite the fact that I see it as absolutely key in deciding how to intervene with any child, adult or family. Along with prompting us to conduct a holistic multi-dimensional assessment, formulation allows us to individualise our understanding of a client, and thus create an individualised intervention which may draw on many models. This ability to individualise our intervention for each person, rather than use one intervention in a one-size-fits-all way, is something I regard as being key to successful interventions and one of the best things about being a clinical psychologist. You can see an outline formulation in Doodle 18.

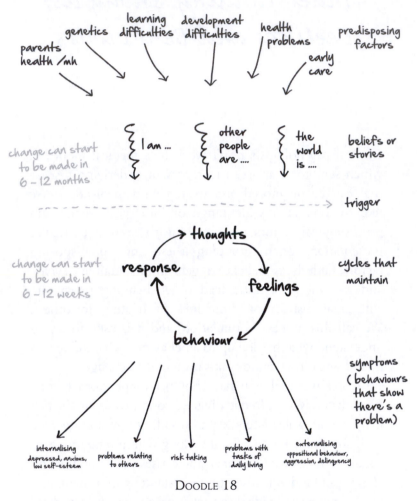

DOODLE 18

Factors like a child's genes, their level of ability, their temperament, any physical disability or learning difficulties are organic examples of predisposing factors. However, early experience will also normally go under this heading because it is something that we cannot change which has a lasting effect on the child. This might include exposure to violence, a lack of early nurture, exposure to excessive criticism and emotional harm, sexual abuse, poor early diet and/or stimulation, exposure to parental mental health problems or drug/alcohol misuse or violence (including whilst in the womb).

These early experiences will lead the child to form a set of core beliefs about how the world is, what other people are like and what they are like as a person. If they have had healthy nurturing experiences and caregivers who have enjoyed being with them and positively reflected what they are experiencing, then the child will build a sense of themselves as being alright or a good person, other people as being mostly kind and well-intentioned and the world as an interesting and mostly safe place. If their experiences are of neglect, chaotic living circumstances, violence, unpredictable or harmful caregivers, criticism, rejection and a lack of positive engagement, then the beliefs they form about themselves, the world and others are very different. They might learn that they are bad or broken or worthless, that other people are dangerous, deceptive or unreliable and that the world is a scary place full of danger.

As I mentioned earlier in the book, these core beliefs have a profound effect on the rest of that person's life, because they determine their self-image, how much they trust others, and how ready for fight or flight they must remain. These core beliefs can also form the rules by which the child believes the world works. For example: 'I am completely bad and when people recognise that they reject me', 'Other people only like me when I meet their needs', 'It is better not to risk trusting others' or 'Other people inevitably let you down.' Once these beliefs are in place, any trigger event or stressor can make them show.

Around the core beliefs is a layer of cycles that maintain the current situation. In their simplest form these are cycles of thoughts, feelings and behaviours within a single individual. For example, if a person is afraid of spiders then they might see one and think, 'Oh no, it's a spider! I can't cope, I must run away and get someone else to deal with it.' They might feel really anxious, and their behaviour might include leaving the room or calling for help so that someone else deals with the spider. Of course that does not allow the person to learn anything new about spiders or increase their ability to cope with them, and so the next time they see a spider the same pattern repeats. As a therapist, the easiest intervention point is in challenging the thoughts about the spider (because, after all, spiders in the UK can't actually do anything bad to people and don't really merit the level of fear and disgust they provoke) and in helping the person to manage their anxiety (by taking deep breaths, for example) and to change their behaviour (stay in the room, have a look at the spider, maybe even catch it with a pint glass and a piece of card and tip it outside the window). Each of these things allows the person to feel more effective and create a less negative cycle.

The other thing that happens with maintenance cycles is that they draw in other people. In the example above, there is someone who will come in and deal with the spider, so that the anxious person doesn't have to. And often despite their best intentions, as in this example, other people's actions allow or reinforce the unwanted behaviour. The behaviours of the individual will also affect the thoughts and feelings of the other person. For example, a child who is reluctant to accept affection might lead the caregiver to have thoughts about the child not liking her/him or perhaps it touches a particularly sore spot of thoughts about being a failure as a parent. These thoughts and feelings might affect how that caregiver is able to behave towards the child. And of course there may be more than one other person, so the thoughts, feelings and behaviours of a partner, your parents, neighbours or teachers might also come into play. This means that when I make a formulation about what is going on for a particular child, I am particularly interested in how their behaviour impacts on other people in their network, and how the behaviour of other people in the network impacts on the child.

CASE EXAMPLE: I never get presents
I worked with an adoptive family who were struggling with having very different expectations of their daughter Elsie when compared with those of her school. The family felt that Elsie (who was about eight years old) was bright, but preferred to act immaturely and put in little effort. So they were trying to encourage her to act more maturely and be responsible for her own choices. They felt that the school, and in particular the classroom support assistant, was quite over-indulgent with Elsie. She would often come home with small gifts, like cuddly toys or dressing-up clothes, or mention having biscuits. Eventually the parents were informed that the school had made a child protection referral. Elsie had told them that her father had hit her and she was scared of him. The parents were very anxious about the child protection process and denied that the reported events had taken place. Social workers who investigated found no evidence to substantiate the allegation.

When I worked with the family and spoke to the school it became clear that Elsie had an insecure ambivalent attachment style, and had found it effective within her family of origin to make others feel sympathy towards her. When her birth mother felt guilty for hitting her she would be given sweets and gifts, and when she looked sad and vulnerable, visitors would give her treats or cuddles. Within the school she had found that telling tales of how deprived she was at home, and how she never got presents, allowed her to get out of activities she did not like and gain second helpings *of pudding, and to get treats and small gifts from her classroom support assistant (who was a doting grandmother to her own family).*

However, it also transpired that the adoptive father was occasionally using smacking[44] as a consequence for challenging behaviour, and this had made her fearful because it reminded her of the assaults she had experienced in the birth family. We were able to work on meeting Elsie's need for nurture, but also to encourage autonomy, in collaboration with the school. We also worked on acknowledging Elsie's past experiences and using effective parenting strategies to build more positive relationships within the family.

In terms of intervention, we know that certain models of therapy can make significant changes to the way people think, feel and behave within 6–12 weeks. Probably the most widely known of these is Cognitive Behaviour Therapy, which is a way of exploring these maintenance cycles, challenging negative thinking and undertaking small experiments to test out the objective truth of certain ideas that the individual believes as incontrovertible truth.

When it comes to changing core beliefs, these are much harder to access and change. Therapy might help to tackle individual symptoms or maintenance cycles, but other symptoms or cycles might continue to emerge to replace them until a very entrenched belief starts to shift. This means that even with skilled therapy, we expect change to only start to be visible in 6–12 months of work. However, the evidence is good that change is possible, and an increasing number of specialist therapies have been developed and researched which have been shown to be effective in changing core beliefs and entrenched patterns of relating to others. These include what are known as the 'third wave' cognitive therapies, such as Schema Therapy,

---

44   Although I do not believe that smacking is a helpful or effective method of shaping children's behaviour, the example given was within the law and thus was something we worked on rather than viewed as a child protection issue.

Compassionate Mind work, Dialectical Behaviour Therapy and Cognitive Analytic Therapy.

When working with parents and children specifically looking at attachment issues, models such as Dyadic Developmental Psychotherapy (which works with parents, and then the parent and child together in a pair or 'dyad'), Theraplay (which uses playful interactions between parent and child), Life Stage Integration[45] and Attachment and Bio-behavioural Catch-up Intervention[46] are starting to show promise. Psycho-educational groups for foster and adoptive parents, such as my group 'Managing Behaviour with Attachment in Mind', have also shown high levels of efficacy in helping caregivers feel more skilled to meet the needs of children with challenging presentations learnt from poor early care, trauma, abuse and neglect.[47] There is every reason to feel optimistic that change is possible, but also to be realistic about the amount of time and effort required.

---

45   See Siegel (2006).
46   See Dozier, Lindheim and Ackerman (2005).
47   See Holmes and Silver (2010).

CHAPTER 12

Parenting with PACE

When I run my groups for adoptive and foster carers, we often talk about how you begin to make up for some of those missed experiences. Dr Dan Hughes, an American clinical psychologist, is someone that I think has been incredibly important in studying how we repair damaged attachment patterns. He is one of the people who has really taught us about the core skills that help to re-parent traumatised children. I went out to America in 2005 to train with him, and it made a huge impact on my way of being as a therapist.

I had always been taught to keep a kind of neutrality with the children, adults and families that I worked with, without showing too much emotion or getting too personally involved. I was persuaded by the historically accepted notion that the best method of therapy was to form a relationship that gradually circled the problem, slowly getting a little closer until the relationship was strong enough to talk about the real business that brought us together. Unfortunately with this technique, a lot of people disengage from therapy or are moved on before you get to the most important bit. Similarly, if carers circle but never speak about the main issues until they know a child really well, the child may end up moving placement before the topic is ever discussed properly.

Dan Hughes turned all this on its head. He said that provided you create certain qualities in the relationship right from the start, you can touch on the main topic of concern very early in the relationship. You can mention it head-on, and then show that the relationship is safe by using ideas of 'break and repair'. So before I explain Dan's main techniques for re-parenting a child whose early care has been damaging, I will explain the idea of break and repair.

As I mentioned in Chapter 5, infants learn to regulate their level of readiness for fight or flight with the help of their parents. At first they need an adult to co-regulate their arousal and recognise what caused those feelings, but this is gradually internalised. By the time children are a bit older we expect them to be able to modulate their own level of physiological arousal because we tell them to have some time out to calm down, sit on the naughty step, or go to their room until they are calmer. With older children we leave that regulation to them more and more.

However, with a child who has not experienced consistent and attuned early care you need to actively repair the relationship each time you break it, in order to build trust that it is the behaviour that is unacceptable to you and that despite the criticism the child is still loved. For the child who has experienced rejection, neglect or abuse any criticism feels like a break in the relationship and you then have to make good that relationship so that the child learns to change the behaviour whilst retaining a sense of themselves as lovable and their relationship with the caregiver being safe. Dan Hughes would add to the arousal regulation the idea that if we tell a child off for what they are doing, we have to help them to regulate, and we have to tell them that the relationship is okay.

From my observations of parents, I think many people do this intuitively with little children. If a toddler touches something they ought not to we say, 'No, no, don't put your fingers in the socket! Come on, let's play over here', which is a break and a repair in very quick succession. What's interesting is that by the time we get to teenagers we often say to them, 'Go to your room and think about what you have done' and we don't actively repair that relationship. We don't actively come back and reprocess that and say, 'You know what, you're a good kid, and you're alright with me. It was just that thing you did that was annoying.' Dan Hughes teaches us that whenever we use a criticism, or whenever the child is in a state of distress, we have to repair that relationship much more quickly and actively if the child has had experiences of trauma or abuse in their background.

CASE EXAMPLE: A very naughty girl!

When I think back to my childhood, there was a time when I was about nine years old where I was very difficult for a babysitter. I refused to go to bed when she said it was bedtime and stayed downstairs no matter what consequences she promised or threatened. When she heard my parents returning from their night out she offered me one last chance to go to bed quickly, offering to tell my parents I had been good and gone to bed at the normal time if I did so. I still refused, and my parents returned to find me downstairs.

I remember thinking they would be very cross with me for being so disobedient, so when my Dad said, 'Go to bed now, we'll deal with you tomorrow', I thought there would be some kind of punishment when I woke up. However, when I woke up life went on as normal. Amazingly, they appeared to have forgotten! So I waited and waited for them to remember and give me my overdue punishment. Hours, days, weeks, months passed. Eventually I asked them about it, fearing I was going to get some long-awaited consequence. My Dad said, 'Oh, I was probably trying to placate the babysitter and just wanted you to go to bed. I don't think I ever intended there to be any more consequence than that.'

I look back on this incident and see that even for a securely attached child who had never experienced abuse or neglect, that little break in the relationship needed to be repaired for me to feel okay about myself and my place in the family. Through that, I can understand how essential it is to provide a repair that is as soon and as obvious as possible for children who have experienced trauma, rejection and maltreatment. It's only normal to have times in which we get angry or we say something critical towards our children, but the important thing is that we give the message that despite this (and even during this) we still love the child as a whole. Dan Hughes recommends 'sixty second scolding' in which you express your frustration for no longer than a minute before repairing the relationship. It sounds like that would be impossible, but a minute is a really long time to try and maintain an angry monologue in practice!

CORE QUALITIES OF A THERAPEUTIC PARENT

As I have said before, the task of re-parenting a child who has been damaged by their past experiences is much more difficult than the task of parenting an untraumatised birth child. I believe that, to be most successful, you need to create certain therapeutic qualities in how you parent that child. Dan Hughes talks about giving a child a PLACE in your home or parenting with PACE.[48] These acronyms allow him to talk about the key qualities of an attachment relationship in which you wish to re-parent a child whose prior care has not been good enough. These qualities, as you can see in Doodle 19, are being Playful, Loving, Accepting, Curious and Empathic. It is useful to think about what each of those things mean in some depth.

We know that some of the best experiences to have in childhood are where people are *Playful* and enjoying your company, and those are the ways for parents to experience and share the positive aspects of interacting with their child. So it is really important to keep the tone playful whenever possible. To use your relationship as an agent of change, you don't want to get stuck in a pattern of criticising or

---

48   See Hughes (2007).

teaching or being aloof and leaving the child to themselves. You really want to get in there and be playing with the child and reflecting back to them how much you enjoy being with them. This doesn't only mean actually doing playful activities with the child, such as using toys or going to the park, but it also includes how you interact with them verbally. When you are playful, you pay attention to what they are experiencing, you interact in ways intended to amuse them and you enjoy being with them. One example

Playful

Loving

Accepting

Curious

Empathic

DOODLE 19

of a very simple game is the 'one two three tickle' game that many parents play with a baby. They establish a rhythm of the count and movement occurring, and then slightly slow it down or speed it up to confound the infant's expectations, and everybody involved enjoys it and shares smiles and giggles and eye contact.

A game can be any form of playful interaction. Playfulness is inherently enjoyable and engaging, and if you can find a playful way to present a task, the child is more likely to comply and produce the desired behaviour. So, perhaps the tidying up which the child would not want to do can be offered as various games and challenges that they might enjoy. Playfulness can make even the most mundane of daily activities into a positive attachment experience. For example, a friend of mine used to wrap her children so they were covered in a large towel after the bath and then say, 'Is this parcel for me? I wonder what is in it? It feels like it might be something lovely like a teddy bear. Oh, it's something soft, and giggly… I wonder what it can be?' whilst feeling and tickling the 'parcel'. Or you can play 'delicious or disgusting' whilst naming items to eat, or you can make a journey in the car pass by playing 'I spy'. You may be talented or uninhibited enough to sing songs together, or fit enough to run around, jump and climb together. Playfulness is about creating joyful shared experience.

To be *Loving* is about showing the child that you enjoy and value them, and are able to provide nurture and empathy. The practical delivery of that is embodied by the other letters in the acronym.

To be *Accepting* is about acknowledging that the child is how they are right now and that you accept the whole of them. You accept the fact that there is a whole lot of traumatic stuff that has gone before, which makes them behave in a number of challenging and different ways, but you consider that the whole child they are right now, complete with all that baggage, is still acceptable and worth loving. That is a really powerful message to convey to a child who may not perceive themselves as lovable or worthy. Given that a lot of children who have experienced trauma, abuse or neglect feel that they are inherently bad people and the cause of their maltreatment, to acknowledge that the child is distressed and carries with them a lot of baggage but to still consider them acceptable as a whole may be something they have never experienced. Several children I have worked with have asked their parents questions like,

'If I broke your favourite vase, would you still love me? If I hurt you, would you still love me? If I killed someone, would you still love me?' to test how far this acceptance goes. There are a few lovely children's books, such as *No Matter What* by Debi Gliori and *Guess How Much I Love You* by Sam McBratney and Anita Jeram, which carry this message in rhyming verse, which shows how universal and significant the experience of being accepted is.

Being *Curious* is about valuing the child's experience and wanting to know how it is from the child's perspective. This might involve actually asking the child about why things are a particular way or, where they are not able to explain, making some guesses to help the child form into words those links between past experiences and present behaviours. This is something we will come back to in more detail later in the book, as it is very bound in with the final core skill on the list – Empathy.

Being *Empathic* is quite challenging as it means really appreciating and understanding what the experience must have been like for your child and conveying that to them. You might speak out what you think their experience is, and what from the past that might relate to. For example, you might say, 'It seems like it is really hard for you when I tell you how wonderful you are. I'm sorry if this is not something you've been told much before you came here.' Or you might say, 'You seem really angry that I've asked you to turn the television off. I wonder if you think I told you to do that because I wanted to spoil your fun?' Provided you do it appropriately and not in a way that will overwhelm the child or place blame at the feet of people they feel loyal to, you can also show your own feelings about the child's experiences, such as your sadness about all the things they missed out on, and your anger at the people who treated them badly. It is not authentic to try to be emotionally neutral with a child who has just disclosed an awful experience.

CASE EXAMPLE: Smile over the sadness

Soon after I trained with Dan Hughes I returned to the UK and was asked to complete an assessment of a teenage girl who had climbed over a safety railing of a multi-storey car park with the intention of jumping off. I asked her all the standard questions about her history and the circumstances of the event, and filled in the risk assessment document as normal. She told me that she had decided she might as well be dead after her mother and step-father had yet another argument. At the end of the explanation she added 'but, you know' and shrugged and smiled. I said, 'I don't know how that is, can you tell me about it?' and she narrated how her drunk step-father had sworn at her mother, thrown his dinner plate at her across the room, then started hitting her mother, who had retreated with her to the bedroom and locked the door. The step-father had then charged the door, breaking the lock, and tipped the bed over on top of them. He had picked up a broken bed leg and started to hit her mother with it. Again the narrative ended with 'but, you know' and a shrug with a smile.

I paused for a while and tried to imagine what it must be like to be 14 and to be in fear of your life and your mother's life, whilst a large angry drunk man beats her in front of you. I felt this overwhelming sense of sadness that anyone should have to experience such a thing. I said to her, 'I'm trying to imagine how that must feel, and I just feel so sad that it's trying to leak out of me, whilst you are trying to smile' and a tear literally escaped as if on cue. The girl looked at me and said, 'Yeah, it's shit isn't it?' and started to cry. The experience was a profound one for both of us. For her she knew I understood her experience, and was authentically there with her and believing her. For me, I felt like I'd skipped to session 20 of the therapy relationship in which we could have tackled the big issues, safe that the relationship was established.

When we think about how to apply braver empathy to the issues around looked after and adopted children, the same kind of approach can apply. Dan Hughes will teach parents to make very brave guesses about what a behaviour might mean, but do so with a playful and accepting tone. One example he told when I trained with him was of two brothers who had been adopted after very serious neglect. The older boy who had been placed at about the age of four was very used to looking after the younger boy who had been placed at about the age of 18 months and he found it extremely difficult in the adoptive home to see the adoptive parents looking after his younger brother.

Dan Hughes described how he did a session with the boy and his parents as a family where he acted out being playful and curious and empathic about what was causing that situation to be challenging. He said to the boy, 'I've been talking to your mum and dad and I've been wondering about how come it is so hard for you to see them looking after your little brother. I'm just wondering about whether it's because you felt like that was your job. You know, it was your responsibility. It was one thing that you had to do to keep you busy and now that has been taken away.' The kid shook his head. So Dan Hughes said, 'Oh gosh, well that's a tricky problem. I'm going to have to figure this out a bit more.' So he thought about it for a while and he said to the boy, 'You know, I'm wondering if it could it be that your job of looking after your brother made you feel like you were really close to your brother, like he and you were together against the world and he was the person you felt closest to. And now it's really difficult to see your mum and dad getting close to him and it feels like maybe you're being pushed a bit further away.' The boy shook his head.

Dan Hughes said, 'Oh well, this really is a tricky problem! I'm going to have to rack my brains about this one. Do you think we are clever enough to figure it out between us? Come on, I'm smart and you are smart, let's think. Could it be that you felt like your brother really needed you and he was someone that really relied on you and that made you feel responsible and important in the world, but now he's learning to rely on other people and it seems like nobody needs you as much.' Again, the kid shook his head. Dan Hughes said, 'Gosh, this is really difficult! How are we going to solve this? So you used to look after your brother and did a really good job of that...' and the boy interrupted him by shaking his head. Dan Hughes said, 'Oh, now I'm finally getting it. You looked after your brother and you did the best job that you could and you thought that was what your brother needed, but now you see your mum and dad looking after him you realise how a kid should be looked after and that what you were doing for him wasn't enough.' The boy started crying, and the mum and dad started crying, because they were in the room to hear it, and all of us who were on the training were probably crying to hear the story because it was so touching and authentic and emotionally raw.

The reason the story is really important and I re-tell it within my groups is because of the fact that Dan made a number of wrong guesses. It's a really good illustration of how a child would have experienced people making wrong guesses. This is important to explore because we're not very brave, we don't like to make guesses until we are sure that they are right. But think about how that child would have felt about Dan Hughes' wrong guesses. Do you think he would have thought, 'That stupid man knows nothing about me' or do you think he would have thought, 'This person is really trying to understand'? I'd say the child is much more likely to experience the latter. And if he's thinking that someone is really trying to understand him, then Dan Hughes has the tone right, because he is being curious, he's being accepting, he's being empathic and the child's experience is that someone really cares and is interested and is helping him make sense of that experience.

Whilst trying to understand, Dan made it clear that the boy had the final say in whether he was right or not. If the child says he is wrong or has misunderstood, he accepts that. We need to take care to be tentative in our guesses so that the child can put us right, and we never interfere with their memories (or risk creating false memories by offering guesses which are forceful or prescriptive). When he gets the right explanation, the boy is very validated by that being an explanation that someone else can understand. It is then a great opportunity for some empathy and comfort to be offered. When a guess about something as emotionally important as this is correct, it is a very powerful experience for everyone involved.

Certainly in my groups for foster and adoptive parents we try to encourage people to be braver in their guesses that they make in order to try and understand the experience of their child. Initially people are quite anxious about trying that out, but when they do try it out they find it incredibly rewarding because when you do get the guess right you feel a closeness and a genuine connection that you may not yet have experienced with the child.

✎ Activity: Empathic guesses

🕉 Having read about the idea of empathy, and making braver empathic guesses, I would really encourage you to try taking it into practice. Good times for empathy are when the child mentions their past, is self-critical, or shows any negative emotions (sadness, anger). Do not try it whilst the child is dysregulated, so if there is a big outburst you may need to practise the soothing techniques I mentioned in an

earlier chapter until the child is calm, and then try some
deeper empathy.

The most important thing you can do to show empathy
is never to dismiss the child's view of themselves. So, if
the child calls themselves stupid, or bad, or worthless or
any other name, resist the Punch and Judy line of 'Oh
no, you're not' and the instinct we've been trained into of
saying, 'You are not a bad child. It's just your behaviour
that is unacceptable.' Try imagining how it feels to be
that child and to believe that as a fundamental truth about
yourself, and see if you can find a way to express that you
empathise with the child's perspective. Although it will feel
uncomfortable to stay with empathy and not immediately
move to adding something hopeful or attempting to problem
solve, it is really valuable for the child to feel understood
and accepted. So, try to say things like, 'I'm sorry that you
feel that way. It must be hard for you to believe that about
yourself. It's brave of you to tell me that you feel that way.
I'm sad that your life experience has taught you that about
yourself' before offering a little of your own perspective,
for example, 'I hope that one day you are able to see some
of the good things about you that I see.'

CHAPTER 13

Layers

If a child mentions a past trauma, do not hesitate to discuss it further. Talking and making sense of these overwhelming experiences helps your child to process them. However, not all children feel able to express all of their past experiences (and what they have learnt to believe about themselves because of them) openly or directly. This can be very confusing, as the child may seem very different in different situations or with different people, or small events may provoke a big reaction. This is something we will come back to in a later chapter, as it may also reflect 'time holes'.

I often draw Russian Dolls as a metaphor for the way we are as people: having lots of different layers that we only reveal as people get to know us better. You will see in Doodle 20 that I have drawn a set of Russian Dolls stacked inside each other. The outer layer represents the face we show to the world. In Russian Dolls the outer layer is the one that is the most decorated, the most painted, the most attractive, so I call that layer 'painted perfect'. It's the mask you want the world to see. In my case that might be trying to be professional or intelligent or punctual or friendly or knowledgeable or kind. It might be slightly different in different contexts but it is the face that you want other people to see.

In the very inside of the Russian Doll is often a sleeping baby doll which is the least well formed, least attractive, least decorated figure and that represents the beliefs you learnt about yourself when you were a baby. Those are the very early beliefs about the nature of yourself, the world and other people, which we discussed in the earlier chapter on formulation. Cognitive behavioural therapists call these schemas, and narrative therapists call them stories, but they are what you believe are the rules by which the world operates, and they underlie everything you think or feel or do. Often for children who have been neglected and abused, their core belief at this level is that they are bad, that they deserve to be (and will inevitably be) treated badly and that the world is full of dangerous people. So beliefs like, 'If people knew the real me I would be abused or rejected' are very common in this group, though the exact words they take on are different from person to person. Core beliefs like this are known as shame and we will talk more about this in the next chapter.

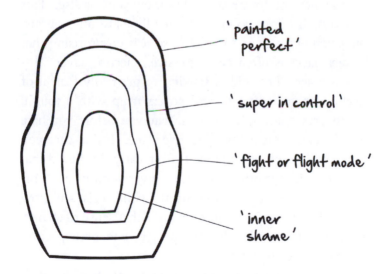

'painted perfect'

'super in control'

'fight or flight mode'

'inner shame'

Doodle 20

The layers between the face you want to show to the world and that core hidden set of beliefs you learnt as a baby act as your defences against the world. So for most young people who have been through trauma, abuse or neglect, the desire is to put on a socially pleasing front, to play the clown, or to desperately try to act like their peers at school. However, this feels quite fragile, rather than authentic, so under any stress you get to see a different facet of their personality.

Normally the one that shows first is what I call 'super in control'. It's a strong desire to take control over the details, to have some say over what other people do, to make life predictable and safe. That is really rational, given the experience many such young people have had of a chaotic unpredictable life in which the adults were not able to provide any sense of order, organisation or safety. However, it tends to have a sense of an implicit threat to it, as if the message conveyed is, 'Do it my way, or else.' This layer says, 'If things go my way they'll be just fine, but just you watch out if they don't!' and so it is unsurprising that the next layer is often an aggressive, rejecting layer. This layer is where the child is starting to get really fearful of rejection or maltreatment and covers it up with a tough, fearless presentation. It says, 'I'll hate you before you hate me, I'll reject you before you reject me.' Inside that you get the raw emotions and beliefs from early childhood that normally spill out only when that anger is burnt off. This is where you get to see how sad the child feels, and how lost and hopeless. They might express that sense of shame, of being a bad and unlovable person, and of expecting maltreatment or rejection.

Many of the young people I see try to be nice, well-behaved, to be what they think others expect them to be, to act as though they deserve good care and to be lovable. However, under stress they find that really difficult so they become very controlling and want to organise things, even things that are not terribly meaningful; they want the same breakfast bowl, to sit in the same place, or they want their mum to do things in a particular way and in a particular order. If that does not work, or if they feel at all criticised or challenged, they come out with being very aggressive and rejecting and enter that fight or flight mode that is really about survival and isn't very logical. All of that masks these inner beliefs about being bad that they desperately want to hide.

Obviously, from individual to individual there may be differences in how these layers present. I've met children who show nothing but anger, as if they have given up on trying to present a pleasing mask to the world. I've also met young people who don't express any anger, as if showing authentic feelings is just too threatening. I've met young people for whom the outer layer is charming, or babyish, or fashionable, or funny, or intellectual. However, it is remarkable how much common ground there is in the overall pattern. Certainly I have shared this diagram with a number of young people (such as teenagers who are testing out risk-taking and rebelling from their adoptive or foster families to see if they can find a sense of more authentic belonging by seeking out the patterns of their family of origin) and there has been a surprisingly strong response to it. I have several times been told by the young person, 'That's it, the thing I can't put words to, that's how I feel' and later been told by the family that this image of Russian Dolls has allowed them as a family to talk about the issue that they now see underlies everything they are going through.

CASE EXAMPLE: Painted perfect

I worked with a young lady of 16 whose adoptive placement was really having difficulties because she was rebelling against their norms and testing out a lot of behaviours that they felt were very risky. For example, she was having some quite unsafe sexual relationships and experimenting with drugs and alcohol and staying out overnight. The referral was triggered because she was doing a number of things that caused concern to her adoptive parents, who then wanted to make restrictive rules and consequences for her. This was a girl who presented absolutely immaculately with the trendiest hairstyle and the most fashionable handbag and shoes and styling. She looked immaculate because she was putting so much effort into her external presentation to try and feel a sense of belonging, but actually her inner core belief was that she was maltreated for a reason and didn't deserve this new life. She felt she was maltreated because there was something bad or different about her that was being hidden. That belief was underlying a lot of her experimenting as to whether she deserved a worse life, and whether people would accept her as a whole if the expectations weren't that she should be painted perfect.

In our first session I drew the Russian Dolls and asked whether it was something she could identify with. She came back to the next session and her parents said, 'She's finally got some words to talk about how she is feeling.' The parents were able to work on giving empathy to the inner beliefs she was hiding, and she was able to show some more authentic fears to her parents. It did not have an immediate impact on her risky behaviour, but with continued empathy she realised that she felt more sense of belonging in her adoptive family when following their norms of expected behaviour than she did when hanging out with more chaotic peers and acting like the stories she was told about her family of origin.

I also think the Russian Dolls are a useful metaphor in terms of the idea of needing to accept the child as a whole. Most people I know who have gone into fostering or adoption want to love that child despite or even because of all of the difficult experiences that child has had, yet most of the children I know are very ashamed of those difficult experiences and want to hide them and pretend never to have had them. So what you get is a child who whenever they are praised is at some level thinking, 'Hah, I've got them fooled with my painted perfect mask' and doesn't believe the compliment to be genuine to them. But whenever you criticise them, even about the most minor thing, the child is thinking, 'Oh shit, they've seen the true me and I might be rejected. They've realised I'm a bad kid and now I'm going to be maltreated.' That's really difficult because it means that all the effort that carers are putting in to help show the good qualities of that child to them are just being brushed off as being false. Praise is just attributed to the surface layer and doesn't sink in, and all the feedback you give to help shape that child to achieve the best possible outcomes in life is seen as criticism that cuts them to the core.

As I said earlier, Dan Hughes talks about how whenever the child reveals a belief about themselves being bad or says anything self-critical, you need to be firstly very empathic by saying things like, 'I'm sorry to hear you think that you are a bad kid. That must be really difficult for you. It's brave of you to tell me that you feel like that. I'm really sad that your life experiences before you came to us made you feel like that about yourself.' The risk in a Supernanny-style response like saying, 'No, no, you're not bad, it's just the behaviour that is unacceptable' is that the child would hear this message as, 'Don't tell me about your inner core beliefs, just keep acting like the painted perfect layer' which means that they continue to feel that their true self is unacceptable to you. To disagree with their belief is also to tell them that the way they perceive the universe is wrong. That would be like me pointing to the sky and saying it's orange; it just doesn't make any sense, so it makes the child think that you're stupid, not that because of their skewed experience they are seeing things differently from the objective truth. It is much more effective to acknowledge the child's perspective as legitimately reflecting their experience, to accept the child where they are with the beliefs they currently hold, and then to offer an alternative interpretation as a possibility.

A core skill in being able to show deep empathy is really needing to accept the child's point of view as being legitimate, even if it is that they are bad and deserve be treated badly. You might notice shame, when the child says something outright that is self-critical, but it might also be that they dismiss a compliment, or avoid eye contact and appear uncomfortable at certain times. Interestingly, we avoid eye contact both when we are ashamed of what someone might see in us, or really worried about what we might see in them. So the child may find it nearly impossible to look at you if you tell them off, as they fear that you have seen the badness inside them and would hate or reject them. But they might also find it very hard to look at you if they think you are being too positive about them when offering praise or affection or hope.

Finding the right balance between accepting the child as they are and allowing them to express their beliefs, and gently challenging them to look at you to check how you are feeling, is one of the skills in sensitive re-parenting. We cannot make our body language and the subtler parts of our facial expression lie, so it can be really helpful to encourage the child to have a really good look at you when you say you love them, or that the fact they did something wrong doesn't mean you are going to reject them, to see if they can make a better judgement of whether it is sincere or fake.

You will become an expert in your child and know their body language, their behaviour and their beliefs. This will allow you to learn when empathy is appropriate. But starting with believing their world view is the mark of true acceptance and empathy, and it will gradually allow the child to tell you more and more about their experience. The more you can offer a sincere experience of empathy, the more understood the child feels and the more their shame becomes something that can be talked about and shared, rather than hidden for fear of rejection. True empathy can be really difficult for us as adults because it brings up a lot of strong feelings, and there may be a strong instinct to move on quickly to problem solving or discussing something more positive. As I mentioned earlier, after the empathy it can be helpful to add a few of your own thoughts about the qualities that you see in the child, and to hope that one day the child can also recognise these.

As I mentioned above, the Russian Doll layers that I draw are just an example of what might be there. They might be in a slightly different order for different people or it might be that the outer layer is painted like a clown or like a very young or ill child who needs a lot of nurture (which we'll come back to in 'Patterns That Suck Us In' later) or it might be that the defences come in a different order. However, the idea of the outer layers being presented in order to get your needs met in a particular way, whilst the negative core beliefs are hidden, is the important aspect of this image. I hope that by thinking about the layers particular children might present, the foster and adoptive carers who come to our group start to recognise them in real life, and respond with greater empathy and acceptance. One of the really core concepts of how to do therapeutic re-parenting is to recognise what these inner beliefs mean, where they come from and what you can do about them, and that leads us on to the idea of shame.

Reflection: Spotting the layers

Take some time to think about your child. What would they want to convey about themselves to their friends, their school, a visitor or to you? What role are they most comfortable in? What would they want to hide? How do they respond to praise? How do they respond to criticism? Have they ever said anything self-critical, or talked about their past experiences? What might they have learned to believe about themselves?

CHAPTER 14

Shame and Changing the Norm

In the last chapter we talked about the fact that a child's early experiences lead them to have certain beliefs about themselves, which often equate to them being a bad person who is unworthy of love and good experiences. This is a very powerful set of beliefs that completely change a child's self-image and the way they view the world. I think Dan Hughes explains shame really well. He draws a shield shape and uses it to illustrate the defences which indicate underlying shame, which is the basis for Doodle 21. He talks about how if a person with underlying shame feels criticised at all, they will tend to deny what they have done as the first defence, then minimise it, then blame it on someone or something else, and then go into rage – getting disproportionately angry.

CASE EXAMPLE: Hitting out
I can think of an example of a session in which I talked to a child called Chloe who hit her cousin, seemingly without provocation, during a family get-together. I asked, 'Why did you hit your cousin?' Chloe responded, 'I never. I never hit her.' (That's denial.) I said, 'Well, you know what, I was talking to your mum and dad and they're pretty reliable people and they saw you hit her, so I'm thinking that you did hit her.' 'Well I didn't hit her very hard, it wasn't a proper hit, she's just a cry-baby.' (That's minimising.) 'Well, you know what? You made your cousin cry and your mum and dad said it

looked pretty hard, so I think we probably ought to talk about what's going on with this hitting.' 'Well, it's her fault. She poked me four times but my mum and dad never see that. They say she's little and so it doesn't count what she does to me. They love her better. They said they wanted a girl like her that was well behaved. They don't care about me. I hate them, they always take her side. I hate her, and I hate them. I wish I was never born.' That's gone straight from blame into rage, and that's when it explodes, which was what the parents had described to me.

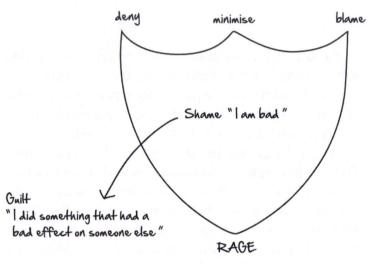

deny   minimise   blame

Shame "I am bad"

Guilt
"I did something that had a
bad effect on someone else"

RAGE

Doodle 21

Dan Hughes would say that going around the shield of shame is a big red flag for the fact that the child is holding core beliefs around being bad. Shame is a belief along the lines of, 'I'm bad, I deserve to be treated badly.' If a child is overwhelmed by shame, that becomes the reason for everything they do: 'Why did you hurt your friend?' 'Because I'm a bad kid.' 'Why did you break that?' 'I'm a bad kid.' It becomes the answer to everything and there is no motivation to change; there is no hope that one day life could be better, as the reason for life being bad is that they deserve it because of some innate qualities. But being overwhelmed with shame is also an egocentric position; it is all about looking inward and blaming yourself, and there isn't any empathy for other people or awareness of the consequences of your actions on others. It is a very immature stage of social development, which children normally pass through in the first two years of life. What we need to do as parents and carers and therapists is to help a child to move from shame towards guilt. Guilt is an outward-facing understanding of what you have done wrong, which demonstrates empathy to others. It says, 'What I did had a bad effect on someone else' and it recognises behaviour as a choice, rather than the inevitable acting out of innate characteristics. That position motivates people to change their behaviour, because they are able to see they have some control and they are suddenly caring about the outcome for others.

This means that one of the times that empathy is at its most effective is when you see shame. As soon as a child does anything that suggests they believe that they are bad or that leads to denial, minimisation, blame or rage, those are the times when we need to find ways of being empathic. Those are the times when we need to be able to regulate our own arousal levels enough to come back with empathy rather than annoyance ourselves (dysregulation). That means that we need to use our support network (the 'tag team' I mentioned earlier) to take over whenever we begin to feel very angry, or to have strong chaotic negative feelings.

Some people ask about whether empathy should be given instead of consequences for behaviour, and if so whether the child will feel that they are being rewarded for their misbehaviour or being allowed to get away with things that are unacceptable. I believe that the ideal response is a mixture of both empathy and consequences. If these are in balance, you are at your most effective as a parent (see Doodle 22). If all you give is empathy, the child's past becomes their excuse for everything they do and change is not necessary. If all you offer are consequences, the child's shame is reinforced; they feel like a bad child and that there is no motivation to change. But if you combine empathy with consequences you can help the child to understand where the behaviour is coming from, why they do it, why it's not okay and how they can change. That is the best of all possible outcomes.

DOODLE 22

It's making that link between past experience and present behaviour that is really important in allowing change to be possible. Dan Hughes uses what I call brave empathic guesses to start offering empathy at times the child is showing shame. So, for example, if a child struggles when you tell them to turn off the television and starts becoming destructive and full of rage, you might say, 'I know it's really frustrating to turn off the television when you are watching something you want to. I guess that it might be if you've had a life like yours that you didn't get to do so many fun things and that the people who interrupted you doing fun things were being mean. I can see why you would find that frustrating. But you know what, when you are a mum, you have to sometimes turn off the television and get the child to do other things so they can learn.

Because I love you and want a really good life for you I really am going to have to keep doing this, even though I know it's frustrating for you.' Every time you have that conversation you are linking the child's feelings to their behaviour, but you are also linking the child's feelings to where they may have come from in their past experience, so it's a really powerful way of applying empathy.

When you give consequences with empathy, the child is often more able to accept them. So, for example, in the case example above about the child who hit their younger cousin, a therapist trained in Dyadic Developmental Psychotherapy might continue on to say, 'Oh, if you feel like your parents don't love you as much as they love your cousin, no wonder you feel so angry with her. That would feel so unfair. I'm wondering if when you lived with your birth mum it felt like that too, that your older sister was much more important and you felt like you got left out of the good stuff and told off much more than her. That would be a horrible thing for you to go through. I'm sorry you experienced that, and I hope that I can help your mum and dad to show you better how much they love you and see good things about you. But you know what? It's still not okay to hit your cousin, so I think you should do something to make it up to her. How about you say sorry to her and play that game that she likes this afternoon?'

The other important thing when considering the balance of empathy and consequence is to be aware (as I mentioned in Chapter 4) that the child might be unconsciously re-creating negative experiences and sabotaging positive experiences. So it might be necessary for you to recognise that pattern and disrupt it. For example, you might say, 'I know that I said you needed to be good this week in order to go to the party on Friday. Well, it seems like we've had a terrible week, and I wonder if part of you felt like you didn't deserve to go to the party. I could keep you at home, but I think you've had enough experience of missing out on nice things. So I've decided that it is more important for you to go to the party and have fun.' Or you might say, 'It seems to me like you are trying to make me angry today. I'm a bit fed up of being angry, so let's try and do something different today. How about we go out to the park, or get an ice-cream?' Some psychologists would call these paradoxical responses, which is a way of saying you do the opposite of what is expected.

Kim Golding[49] reminds us of the value of preserving a positive family atmosphere, and actively choosing to take the more enjoyable option so that as a family you are able to have more positive shared experiences. This is not only important for the child, who may have missed out on a lot of normal enjoyable experiences, but also for the family, who also deserve to have positive experiences of being together. It is helpful to find ways to have fun and focus on the positive parts of the relationship, even when the child's behaviour can at times be draining and emotionally exhausting (and seem to keep you in a punitive position as a caregiver, which is something we will return to in Chapter 17).

CASE EXAMPLE: *Making the ordinary extraordinary*
I went to visit a girl called Elouise in her foster placement, about five months after she was removed from her family of origin. I asked her to tell me about what was different in the house. She showed me how they had a garden where they grow some vegetables, and she had her own room with pink bedding. Elouise told me she had the 'best ever day out' when her carer had taken her to a large garden centre where they had been able to look at the fish and pets, and stopped for a drink and some cake in the café. The foster

---

49   See Golding (2008).

carer told me how Elouise had found it almost impossible to be bought new things, unless the carer bought enough that each of her siblings (placed elsewhere) could have one before she did. When bought a party dress, Elouise had been shaking and crying with delight to try it on, as she had never had anything so pretty and brand new before. She had then said to the foster carer, 'I promise I will keep it nice and clean so that when my mummy gives it to my sister she will still think it is a new dress.' It was inconceivable for Elouise to imagine that she deserved something nice in her own right. In her experience everything in life was rationed and she was the lowest priority in the queue after her mother and her four siblings.

She was very worried that if she felt or expressed affection to the foster carer, this would mean that she loved her birth mother less. This was very understandable as she came from a world where everything, including attention and affection, was in such short supply and not always available. I talked to Elouise and her foster carer about how love is not like a cake, where the more people you cut it up for the less any person gets. Love is like candles, where the more you light the more light there is for everyone. As Elouise stayed in the placement she began to be able to accept the normality of life in the foster family, that being read bedtime stories, or given medicine when she felt ill, were things that she deserved. The social worker described her as 'opening like a flower' in the new environment, and the court was able to recognise the need for Elouise to be adopted into a family where she could be the centre of attention. She was not placed with her siblings, although regular ongoing contact was arranged.

Similarly, I was really struck by going to hear a talk about ChildLine, the charity that children can ring if they want to report abuse or distressing experiences. One of their early calls was from a girl who rang up and said, 'I feel really stupid calling, but the other girls in my class tell me that children do not usually sleep on the garage floor on newspaper.'

It really goes to show how strongly normative our own experiences become; that every person believes that their life experiences are commonplace until they start recognising through broader experiences outside their family of origin that what they experienced is not how it happens elsewhere. Obviously, this can only happen when you have other experiences to compare and contrast with, and for many children this process only begins when they are removed from their family of origin. Initially they think that the family they are placed in is the exception to the norm and not vice versa. When coupled with a strong sense of shame and not deserving positive experiences it can be very hard for young people whose whole world was made of experiences that most people would consider to be dysfunctional to re-norm themselves.

Reflection: Visiting the unfamiliar

Have you ever visited a different household or a different part of the country (or a different part of the world) and noticed how different the day-to-day sensations are? Think about somewhere you have been that felt different. Was it louder/quieter? Did it smell different? Were there more or fewer people? Did the people behave differently? Were there different plants or animals around? Was the landscape and colour palette different? How did it make you feel in your body? Were you more tense or more relaxed?

Hopefully this will help you to think about how it must be for children to change their expectations when they change placements. We will come back to some strategies to increase children's sense of belonging in the next few chapters.

CHAPTER 15
Roles and Belonging

Each of us is influenced by a number of societal and family expectations about roles. We have a sense of what is required of us that is determined by our age, our gender, our culture, our religion, our peer group, our profession, our appearance, any disability or difference from the norm, and numerous other factors. We also have expectations of what it means to have our position within the sibling group (e.g. to be the oldest, the middle child, the baby of the family) but also to have our particular traits (e.g. to be 'the helpful one', 'the practical one', 'the ditzy one', 'the funny one', 'the naughty one' or 'the clever one'). These roles or stereotypes have huge influence on how we understand ourselves and anticipate how others will interact with us.

For example, as an older sister I was brought up believing it was a positive characteristic to look after others, and I learnt to be more practical and assertive than my younger brother. As I grew older, people listened to what I had to say, so I started to believe that what I said was interesting. It is no surprise given this context that I remained in education a long time and then went into a 'helping profession' in which I do a lot of talking, but can also apply practical skills or assertiveness when necessary!

Interestingly, the labels that we apply to people easily become a self-fulfilling prophecy. In several scientific studies, pupils' attainments have been shown to be heavily influenced by the expectations of their teachers and parents.[50] If a sample of children are selected randomly and flagged to their teacher as having hidden potential, their scores will go up compared with their peers over the course of the following year. Where we expect children to misbehave, they often fulfil the expectation. Parental expectations and the way parents treat their children are immensely powerful in determining the outcomes for those children.[51] Changing the way parents treat their children changes what these children achieve dramatically, for example the 22 million children who received the Head Start programme over the last 50 years.[52]

When we look at children who have been rejected within their family of origin, or blamed for placement breakdowns, we see young people with disorganised attachments. Those are the children with the major behaviour problems, the self-harm, the 'manipulative' and 'attention-seeking' behaviour, the ones more vulnerable to being victims of further abuse and with problems that follow them into adulthood. This can mean they re-create (unintentionally) the very things that have already scarred them in their adult lives and for their own children. They hold a strong sense of the chaos and rejection being their fault, and no matter where they go they take this with them.

I tend to think of an image from the film *Spirited Away* (a Japanese animation by Hayao Miyazaki, from Studio Ghibli) which captures the different ways of seeing very troubled children. There is a scene in which the main character,

50   See Davis-Kean (2005) and Rosenthal and Jacobson (1968).
51   Negative parental appraisals lead to an increased chance of negative behaviour. See Matsueda (1992).
52   Interventions like Head Start make a massive change to outcomes. See Mills (1998), Welsh and Farrington (2007), Zagar, Busch and Hughes (2009) and Zigler and Muenchow (1994).

a young girl called Sen, is working in a bathhouse for the spirits. A giant stink spirit arrives, illustrated as a huge putrid slug trailing disgusting black gloop, who wants to use the baths. No one is willing to assist him because of the smell, so Sen is sent in to run the baths. As she runs the water, she notices that the stink spirit appears to have a large splinter. She attaches a rope and helps to pull it out. Out comes a broken bicycle, followed by other items of rubbish and pollution until the room is filled. Once the mess and water clears it becomes apparent that the stink spirit has transformed into a beautiful river spirit. He had been disguised by years of pollution that had been thrown into the river, but once this is separated from him he is able to realise his true form again.

I tend to think that a lot of the children I meet have been polluted by their life experiences and are unable to show their full potential because of this. As we treat them well and show them that they deserve a better life, they are able to disclose and sift through all the negative experiences that have changed them in the safety of a supportive relationship. Gradually they are able to show us glimpses of their true form – the child they would have been if they had only experienced secure care and positive role models in their life. However, at first they are good at using their most disgusting learnt qualities to keep people away.

Reflection: Roles

Have a think about the roles that different people in your family took. What influenced your development? What roles did you have to fit in with? What impact has that had on your development? Did you like the roles assigned to you or did you rebel against them? What was the role of a parent in your experience?

Now think about the role expectations that might

have been there for your child in their birth family. What was expected of them? What were their parents like? How were they thought of? How about since they arrived in your family? What roles do they like and dislike? What labels have they attracted? Do they take on different roles in different contexts?

It is interesting to think whether the role people take on is one of a number of facets of their personality, or whether it is the only aspect of them that other people see. I know that when I am in different environments I show different facets of myself. For example, when people read what I have written for psychology graduates or people training in clinical psychology I am perceived by them to be a sort of stern and serious character. But if they come to an event where they can meet me or hear me speak they often comment about me being younger, more cheerful or less scary than they expected! Within my family I might be perceived as the one who is good at problem solving and helps out other people, but that can make it difficult for others to recognise when I am struggling and could do with a bit of help.

CASE EXAMPLE: *The naughtiest boy in the naughty boys club*
I worked with a young lad called Ernest who prided himself on being the naughtiest boy in his school and on the estate where he lived. He found it very hard to stay still and often ended up in trouble and getting punished both at home and at school. He had a list of stories about his adventures and the consequences of these, which he would retell with great relish to anyone who would listen. When Ernest's adoptive parents came to see a colleague and myself in clinic, he was unable to stay in the room. He wandered out into the car park, so I followed him and started to talk to him. He seemed somewhat surprised that I didn't seem to mind that he was outside, and was somewhat baffled when I suggested that he try to climb one of the small trees in the planted area adjacent. He was unable to reach the lower branches, so

I made him a step up with my cupped hands, and he climbed up so his feet dangled down near my face.

I said it was brave of him to trust me to make a step for him, and he acknowledged that he felt I might be trustworthy. I asked him if it was scary to be up high, and he said it was a little bit. I said that lots of people I work with have had experiences that are scary, and Ernest said that he had seen scary things where he lived before. I asked if it was scary where he lived now. He told me that it was a little bit, because his adoptive mum was poorly, and he had been told that the reason he couldn't live with his birth mother was that she was poorly, but that people really meant she was using drugs. He was quite worried that his adoptive mother might not be able to look after him, and that he didn't quite know what was wrong with her. We made an agreement to go and find out this information, and it transpired she had had a recent hysterectomy. We were able to talk with Ernest about the differences between what happened to his birth mother because of her drug addiction and what was currently happening to his adoptive mother. I was able to explain about fight or flight, and talk about how being 'naughty' felt stronger and safer than being scared. This allowed the adoptive parents to respond to the unexpressed need and offer reassurance, rather than thinking of him as self-sufficient and challenging.

BELONGING

I would like also to think about the idea of belonging, because an adoption or long-term foster placement is like an arranged marriage where there isn't always an immediate sense of love or fitting together comfortably (though like arranged marriages, the majority of relationships work out quite well in the end, provided they are approached with the right attitude). Perceived belonging is an incredibly powerful sense we have in different environments, as to whether we feel comfortable and at ease, or tense and awkward or able to only show one facet of ourselves.

When I run groups for foster and adoptive carers and for professionals, I often get people to think about times in their own life when they have had a very strong sense of belonging or not belonging. People have talked about particular social clubs, particular areas that they have lived in, moving from one area to another with a particular accent, moving from one country to another or working in particular work places, belonging to particular professional groups or being involved in sporting activities or military activities; a whole variety of different examples. However, the examples all seem to boil down to similar core experiences.

When we talk about what gives a sense of belonging, it is often about looking the same as others in the group, having a common language and common experiences with other people and feeling that you are like them in some way and that they know you well enough to treat you in a way that you like to be treated. When you belong you know people's nicknames, you know the shared jokes, you know the story and the history, you feel accepted and things are familiar. You feel safe and as if you have a particular defined role that you feel confident in fulfilling. When people have a strong sense of not belonging it is often the case that they feel left out of the group because they are not aware of those shared jokes, or the shared language or the nicknames, or feel uncertain of their role or of their value to others. They may have experienced teasing for things that are different or people who have not recognised their efforts, or may feel that there are unclear expectations or that they are not known as an individual.

Looked after and adopted children often have a strong sense of not belonging. It is difficult to give an experience of belonging to a new person when they come to your home.

Unlike the people you have lived with for a long time, you will not know what their favourite breakfast cereal is or whether they are a morning person or an evening person or an outdoor person or a home body, or whether they like to be very social or have a lot of quiet time to themselves. It is difficult to be able to tell straight away the stories and the history of all the names and all the things that are going on in your household. Similarly, it takes time to put up pictures of the child in the home, and to adapt their environment to their tastes.

I remember when I met my parents-in-law for the first time they had a number of words, phrases and nicknames that were completely unfamiliar to me. For example, it would not be surprising to get a greetings card signed 'from me and Boot' from my in-laws. I still to this day do not know the story that makes my father-in-law's nickname Boot, but other words I have come to learn the story about. For example, they call instructions 'strollers' because my husband as a small boy could not pronounce 'instructions' and they thought his replacement was charming enough to continue. In their household they also do a number of activities differently from my family. So, for example, they have a very flamboyant, extravagant Christmas with huge numbers of presents, most of them surprises, whereas in my family Christmas was very low key and people could suggest a present they would really want, or ask someone else what they would like to be given.

These subtle but pervasive differences are between two white British households where the family members are of similar ages and levels of income. When we have friends to stay who come from more diverse backgrounds, more things diverge from their expectations. If you cross cultures or religions, then this also impacts. To try to imagine what it must feel like for a young person to move from a chaotic household with lots of siblings, and partners of their mother coming and going, in the midst of a council estate, into an adoptive home in the countryside where they are the only child, is mind-blowing for me. Yet children are placed in all kinds of family configurations and matching cultural placements are not always available.

Reflection: Building belonging

Think about the differences between your child's lifestyle in their family of origin and their lifestyle now. What has changed? Are there any things that seemed unfamiliar to them? To what extent were you able to find out about their typical daily routine, or their normal environment before they came to you? Is there anything you could do to increase their sense of belonging (e.g. putting up their photos with the ones you have on display of your family, or allowing them to customise their bedroom)? Does their life story book, if they have one, include arriving at your home? If they don't have a life story book, can you make one together, perhaps with the help of the child's social worker?

Sometimes building belonging takes a long time and a lot of effort, and sometimes it happens almost by accident. 'Click' is the word used within the adoption research literature to describe the moment at which there is a sense of the child belonging within the family. Sometimes there are the most incredible stories that connect the child with their new family, whether it be a liking for Marmite and banana sandwiches, or having a similar surgical scar to the adoptive or foster father. These little links can be incredibly powerful. However, they need to be told as a family story that uses the little links as examples of why you belong together.

CASE EXAMPLES: Click

I have been told a few amazing examples of 'clicks' during my professional life. One couple told me that they were trying for a baby when they moved to a new house. When they replaced the carpet they found a section of the concrete floor on which a young child had written 'Chris, age 5' and drawn a smiley face. They wished intensely for the kind of child who could have done that. Several years later, they decided to adopt a child and when they were approved they went to an event where video clips were played of children who were waiting for adoption. They were very attracted to a little boy with glasses and a mischievous grin, whose name was Chris. He moved in with them just after his fifth birthday.

Another couple told me how they had expressed interest in a girl they saw on a video clip, with curly red hair. When the social worker had come round to visit to provide them more information about this child, the soon-to-be-adoptive-mother showed her a photograph. The social worker asked her how she had already obtained a photograph of the girl they wished to adopt. The lady explained that it was not a photograph of the girl, but a 50-year-old image of her own mother during childhood.

These kinds of stories can be told to the child to illustrate how they belong in the family, but it can also be very mundane things that are used to make the same point, for example, being 'musical like mummy' or 'a natural gardener like daddy', 'bossy like mum', 'tall like dad' or liking/hating Marmite or early mornings like other members of the family. Notice which parts of their appearance or mannerisms are similar to other members of the family. Talk about 'in our family we…' when explaining rules, ideas and beliefs about the world (e.g. 'in our family we try to be kind to others').

CHAPTER 16

Stories

One of the other techniques that is really helpful in re-parenting children who have been exposed to chaos and trauma and abuse is to use stories. Lacher, Nichols, Nichols and May have written a book called *Connecting with Kids through Stories*[53] which has some really good examples of how to do this, and one of the things that they talk about are 'claiming narratives'. Claiming narratives are a very powerful way of telling a child about what they deserved in their early life, and helping them interweave their story with yours. So you can talk about first of all what was going on in your life at different points in the child's life. For example, 'We got the dog when you were two years old' or 'We planted that tree around the time you were born' or 'We got married four years before you were born.' You might want to explain that you moved to this house when they were this old or went on this holiday when they were that old, or show them your photograph albums and relate the dates to events in their life.

Sharing your stories gives ownership of that background experience to that child. So if another child in the playground says, 'I'm going to Disneyland in the summer', instead of that being completely foreign (as foreign as the tea and cake game is to someone who has only learnt the beer game), they can say, 'My mum and dad went to Disneyland when I was two' or 'My mum and dad went

---

53   See Lacher *et al.* (2012).

to America the year before I was born.' Although it's not in the child's own repertoire, they will have a connection to more of the experiences within their new peer group if they have woven your stories into their own.

So the first thing about these narratives is that they interweave the child's story with your story, and that's really powerful as they find connections and common ground that their securely attached peers would identify with. But the second and most important thing that happens with a claiming narrative is that you tell the child about the life that they deserve, and the life you would have given them if you had been their caregiver from the start. You might want to tell the child this story in many parts and with increasing levels of detail if they are interested.

For example, you might tell them, 'I would have been so excited to have been pregnant with you! Your dad and I would have been so careful about what I ate all the way through the pregnancy and we would have started decorating the spare room and getting all the baby things. We would have been so excited to tell the news to granny and granddad and we would have gone out and bought baby shoes and little babygros and nappies.' You might want to actually take the child and show them those things in a baby shop or to buy some of those things to show the size of them and how small they are and how fragile a baby is. You might want to continue the story, explaining, 'If I was pregnant with you and nearly ready to give birth, I would have been this big [gesture with arms]. Come and curl up in front of me and let's see if daddy can get his arms all the way round. You would have been inside my tummy and I would have been so excited thinking you were going to arrive.'

Using this story as an example may feel inappropriate if you are a foster carer (particularly if the placement is short-term), or be very difficult if you have adopted because of being infertile or after a difficult history of pregnancy, so you may wish to start with the new-born stages, or the earliest that you can comfortably talk about with the child.

For example: 'When you arrived you would have been so small and fragile, I would have been a little bit scared to hold you and I would have looked after you so carefully. Whenever you cried I would have gone to see what it was. I would have been so anxious about whether you were breathing right and I would have wanted you to sleep in my room. I would have been so careful about what I fed you and I would have kept you really safe and I would have made your room all nice and warm.' You can make the story as elaborate as you want, provided the child is interested, and you can emphasise areas in which their care was lacking to show what should have been provided. It can be worth referring back to the wall exercise and thinking about which bricks are missing for your child, as these are the things you should detail in the claiming narrative.

This is a really clever technique because it does not criticise the child's parent who they might be loyal to by saying everything that they did was wrong. It simply describes how you would have parented them given the opportunity.

The child can then compare this to their actual experiences, and use this as a reference point to understand what 'normal' or good enough care is like. It is really important to demonstrate to children that they deserve to have good care, otherwise they will continue to associate the poor care they received with something innate about themselves, which in their mind means they deserve that level of care.

Reflection: Changing life

At a very trivial level you can imagine a small facet of what it must be like for children to move from one set of life experiences to another by imagining what it would be like if someone told you to brush your teeth before or after breakfast (whichever is the opposite to what you currently do). I know for me it would feel really uncomfortable to leave it as long as brushing my teeth after breakfast, but for some people the idea of having eaten breakfast and left your mouth dirty from breakfast would be equally uncomfortable.

Now imagine that you are a child and you are going from one household in which things are done in one way to another household in which many different little detailed things are happening in a completely different way to the way you have always believed was the only way, the normal, the right way of doing things. It would be very hard to adjust. I can only liken it to the experience of beginning to read a book and learning all the characters' names, the plot, the setting, all of the beginnings of the story and then starting chapter four and it having a different cast, a different setting and a different set of events happening. It would not make much sense, and you would be waiting for the time in which something connected the two experiences in order to feel that it was one coherent book. These young people have skipped from reading chapters one, two and three in their birth family to chapters four and five in a foster home, maybe chapter six in a different foster home, and maybe only when they got to chapter seven are they in their permanent home. It must be very difficult to make sense of who these people are and the way the world works.

Using claiming narratives starts to interweave the story that came before and the way that you are doing things now. It also becomes a way of showing the child that you really want them to belong. You can also project the story into the future by talking about what will happen when they start big school, when they finish school, when they start a job, when you all go on holiday, when you reach Christmas and all the future points that give a child confidence that they will not have already moved on somewhere else by then.

The same book also has some useful techniques for using stories as metaphors for the experiences that children have been through and we have found that very helpful with some young children. A colleague of mine, Dr Natalie Briant, was particularly creative at writing these kinds of stories with families, and the following are stories that we wrote together for particular children.

CASE EXAMPLE: *The cat who was only a kitten herself*
Natalie wrote a story that I adapted when working with a child called Angel who was six years old and from a family where the birth mother was very young and had learning difficulties, and kept returning to a violent alcoholic partner, despite spending time in a mother and baby unit and various refuges. Angel remembered her mother as loving and could not understand why she had been 'rescued' into an adoptive family but her mother had not been.

THE CAT WHO WAS ONLY A KITTEN HERSELF
Once upon a time there was a kitten who lived in a barn on a farm. She met a big tough tomcat and got pregnant, but she was only a kitten herself, so she didn't know how to look after the new kittens that arrived when she gave birth. She tried to keep them clean, but the barn was very messy. She tried to feed them, but there wasn't much to eat. The tomcat would go out and try to hunt things for them to eat, and sometimes he got some food, and sometimes he didn't. Sometimes he would drink water from the dirty puddles and it would make him feel a bit funny, and he would come back

and hurt the cat who was only a kitten herself and scare the babies, but she felt safer when he was around, as the barn was kind of scary.

One day the farmer came into the barn and saw the cat who was only a kitten herself and her baby kittens. He could see that they looked hungry and scruffy and scared, so he took them into the farmhouse. In the farmhouse they got saucers of clean milk, and some tasty food every morning and night. It was nice and warm and safe, but the cat who was only a kitten herself didn't know how to live in a farmhouse. She only knew how to live in a barn, so one day she ran off back to the tomcat in the barn. The farmer wanted to help her, but he couldn't keep her inside if she didn't want to stay, so all he could do was to keep looking after the baby kittens.

The baby kittens missed their mummy and wished she would stay in the house, but they didn't want to go back out to the scary cold barn again. They liked the other animals in the farmhouse, and the farmer and his wife were very kind to them, so they knew that they could have a good life there.

CASE EXAMPLE: The jungle lion moves to the plain
I worked with a young girl whose mother had been very flamboyant at certain times and very self-neglectful in the lows in between in which she had let her hair get matted and would stay in bed for days at a time. The mother often had very unsafe partners around, some of whom had made sexual approaches to the children or been physically aggressive to them. They had had a very chaotic household with a large sibling group and other people coming and going at all times. After a non-accidental injury the children were removed and placed into a number of separate placements. Netwe, the eight-year-old daughter from that family, really struggled with being moved from that household to a very quiet, calm foster placement in which she was the only child. She had also been very insistent on wanting to wear high heels and short skirts and make-up; I think to mimic her mother's higher times.

You will remember that this is not an uncommon pattern. When you are used to the emotional volume being very high, it seems eerily quiet in these low emotional volume homes that children are placed in for adoption and fostering. But for the adoptive and foster parents, the child's emotional volume seems incredibly loud and out of place, and it is difficult for those two things to adjust together. In my experience it takes really quite a long time for the child's arousal levels to come down to match the parents, a fact confirmed by research.[54] So we wanted to write a story to help the child make sense of this in metaphor form.

We wanted to use a metaphor of jungle animals, and Natalie had the brilliant idea of a lion cub using mud to paint on herself. Here is the story we created.

THE JUNGLE LION MOVES TO THE PLAIN

In the jungle, pride life was very busy and noisy. There were a lot of cubs in the den and there were lots of lions and other animals around. The hyenas would come and join in with the pack. They would laugh and seem fun during the day but at night time they were quite scary and would snap their teeth and often hurt the cubs when no-one was looking. After a hyena hurt the girl cub, she was sent to live with other lions far away from the jungle on the plains. When the girl cub moved from the jungle to her new home with the plains pride she found it very strange. She was the only cub in the den with two grown-up lions and it seemed very quiet. There weren't any hyenas around and not so many other animals to play with either. The girl cub found it hard to fit in because nobody knew the games she had played in the jungle. But she really wanted to try to make friends and belong in the plains pride. So she went out and looked at who the other animals seemed to like. Everybody liked the leopard, who seemed really confident even though she didn't have a pride at all, so the lion cub decided she wanted to be like the leopard. She went down to the river and found some dark brown mud. She dabbed on paw prints and spots all over her back like a leopard to see if she could fit in better. But when the other animals saw her new pattern everybody teased her and laughed, so she went down to the watering hole and cried. The elephant came down to the watering hole and asked the girl cub, 'Why are you crying?' and she said, 'Because I wanted everybody to like me and play with me, so I painted on spots to be like the leopard, but even

---

54   Mary Dozier, an American professor of psychology, has been doing research where she swabs parents and children for cortisol. She has been tracking what happens to cortisol patterns in different forms of placement. It is fascinating work and quite complex, but it is really confirming that arousal levels only begin to normalise when you have been quite a long time in a very predictable low emotional volume home, and that change is pretty slow. She has been developing interventions to maximise this.

then nobody liked me.' The elephant was very wise and he said to her, 'The other animals like the leopard because she is kind and fair and honest, not because of her spots. If you are kind and fair and honest, other animals will like you too. But it will take some time.' When she followed the elephant's advice, the girl cub learnt to get along better with the other lions. Gradually, she made friends with the other animals that lived on the plains and began to enjoy life living in the plains pride.

The story acts as a metaphor for the child's experience, and can be evolved according to the child's response to it. For example, if Netwe had said, 'The hyenas used to squash the cubs so they couldn't breathe' that would be a really helpful disclosure about her past experience that could be built into the story.

The stories you write and tell can also reflect different aspects of the child's experience. This can be their current or future experience as well as metaphors for their past trauma. So, for example, Natalie wrote a story about a car that was stuck in reverse for a boy who was oppositional. The story gave empathy for the pattern he had learnt, but also showed how he could benefit from sometimes choosing to do as he was told. Other stories can be written to prepare for a successful future, whether this is in terms of explaining what happens when we go on holiday, or imagining being a grown-up and still within the family.

✎ Activity: Telling stories

🖈 Think about the messages you would like to convey to your child. Try to write a story to tell your child that conveys these messages. The easiest place to start is with a 'claiming narrative' that interweaves their milestones with events in your life, and tells the child how you would have cared for them if given the opportunity. See if you can write a short story about this to tell to your child.

✦ You will need to find the right opportunity to tell the story. Perhaps it can be at bedtime, or when the child is sitting on your knee on the sofa, or is wrapped up snug in a blanket, or is stuck in the back of the car for a long journey. Tell a fairly short simple story, and allow the child to ask for expansion if they want (or you can tell more if they seem interested). If the child does not seem interested, or is physically active or not making eye contact, keep telling the story. Sometimes the content of the story will raise the child's physiological arousal and means they need to fidget or be active, but in my experience they will still be listening!

CHAPTER 17

Time Holes and Triggers

The concept of 'time holes' is a really useful idea that was first described by Angela Hobday, a clinical psychologist with a lot of experience personally and professionally of adoption and fostering. She talks about a time hole as being a useful image when a young person's reaction in the present is disproportionate to what is going on in the present. So, for example, if you ask a child to turn off the television and that leads to a rage where they are attacking you or destroying their toys or pulling out their hair or screaming and sobbing in a corner, that would be disproportionate to the present trigger, and would almost always relate to something in the past. Angela Hobday would use the image of falling through a time hole to describe how that response to the situation comes from the past. I have illustrated this in Doodle 23.

Small trigger

reaction to past trauma

DOODLE 23

CASE EXAMPLE: 'Ugh, you're disgusting!'

I worked with a foster family where a boy called Mike had been with them for four years. He had a very neglectful early background and he had been a boy who was allowed to get very dirty and was often sent to nursery with a full nappy and stained clothing. Because he was dirty and smelly, other children had come to regard him as very unattractive to play with, so he had been very left out and scapegoated. The staff at nursery had often tried to clean his clothes and change him, to make life nicer for him, but this was insufficient to keep him in a presentable state. When I worked with the foster family they told me that Mike was having rages that had no apparent trigger.

I asked them to tell me about the last time before our appointment that Mike had gone into a rage. They told me: 'It was a really lovely day in which several friends of the family had come over with their children and everybody was eating jam doughnuts. It should have been a really lovely time but Mike went off in a rage and ruined it.' I asked them to unpick that for me and tell me exactly what was going on. They told me that Mike had bitten into his jam doughnut and a splodge of jam had fallen out on to the table. As many of us might do in the privacy of our own homes, Mike had used the doughnut to scoop up the jam that had dropped and had carried on eating. Someone else at the table had said, 'Ugh, you're disgusting!' and pointed their finger at Mike. That had been the trigger for an extreme rage in which he had knocked everything off the surfaces in the dining room and had gone up to his bedroom and started smashing the toys that they had given him for his birthday.

It was really clear to see with the idea of time holes that being pointed at and described as disgusting was a very powerful trigger for Mike to feel what he had felt when he was the little boy who was neglected and smelly and dirty and nobody wanted to play with him. He felt like he did not deserve a good life, so what he had done was to destroy all the trappings of the good life he had now been given, by knocking everything off the surfaces to make a mess and destroying all the toys that he did not think he deserved. This is an incredibly powerful reaction to something, which really makes sense when you understand the history but makes no sense with only the information available in the here and now.

Angela Hobday herself talked about handing out packets from a multipack of crisps. I am sure you can picture the scene of different people in the household asking for ready salted or salt and vinegar or cheese and onion or smoky bacon flavour as she was throwing the packets of crisps from the multipack. She said that when she threw a packet of crisps for one of her daughters, she cowered. Angela said that she suddenly realised she had learnt something new about her daughter; that at some point in her history, before she had been in their family, someone had thrown things at her which hurt her.

So time holes are a really powerful concept and they are a great opportunity for empathy. If you can help the child to connect the experiences that led to the feelings that led to the behaviour, you can help them understand why they feel and behave the way that they do. This allows them to view themselves in a different way. It does not just become a reinforcement of shame that they are a bad child and that they did something with no reason. It becomes part of their increasing ability to apply that frontal lobe thinking that connects cause and effect and makes life into a coherent narrative in which you can change how you think about things or how you behave, in order to get different experiences and to have the better experiences in future.

It is also useful to think about sensory triggers. Early trauma may be remembered in terms of bodily sensations and a reminder of those sensations can suddenly take them back to the trauma. At those times the child may be cut off from their ability to look at their experiences verbally or cognitively and may be immersed in debilitating fear or shame. Painful and frightening memories may have been pushed aside but still disturb the child and their relationships. Reminders of trauma could be in the form of smells, sounds, textures, tastes, tone or pitch of voice, or any other memory. I have had children talk about how they associate the toast popping out of the toaster with the domestic violence incident that led to their father's arrest and their removal into Care. I have had a child who was struck with fear whenever they heard the sound of someone stirring their tea, as their sadistic grandfather was the only person in their household to take sugar. I have met children who associate the texture of raw egg white with sexual abuse. It is fairly common for certain ages and one particular gender to trigger a more fearful response, or for it to relate to particular characteristics – glasses, or the smell of a particular perfume, or overweight women.

It is also really common for children to learn to play out a different pattern with different members of the family. So, for example, they might be really difficult and oppositional with their adoptive mother and act in ways which make her feel inadequate or angry, but they might be playful and compliant with their adoptive father. This can make it really tricky for the other adults to empathise with how the primary carer is feeling, as they only see much more positive patterns from the child. This can put strain on relationships, where one person feels blamed or inadequate because the child is more difficult with them, or feels that the other adult doesn't understand. It may also be that one adult falls in love with the child, whilst the other doesn't have the same feelings straight away. Or it might be that one person is somehow repulsed by something the child does, whether that is the sudden exposure to bodily fluids and mess that young children bring, or the discomfort of a sexual undertone to the way a child behaves.

When these 'splits' happen, it is really important to talk about your different experiences and to consider where the different patterns originate, and what echoes they have in your own life. Certain things are much more loaded if you have had certain experiences yourself. So, for example, I have met several adoptive and foster carers who have been really bothered about whether or not a child could have been sexually abused, and find it incredibly hard to deal with any hint of sexualised behaviour, because of experiences in their own lives. Similarly, some carers find themselves getting really angry with a child who is rude or ungrateful or always wants the last word, if these were things that were against the rules in their own childhood, whilst their partner might not be bothered at all.

Another situation that can be very destructive within a placement is if a child makes allegations against someone within the family. It is very difficult to balance trusting the child and taking seriously their allegations whilst also protecting someone that you know and care about. Even where allegations are clearly false and can be rapidly dismissed by the professional network, it can feel like a huge betrayal and be very hard to have continued empathy for the child. However, it is worth bearing in mind that a lot of children who have experienced abuse have tried to make disclosures in the past and not been heard or believed. Thus when their relationships and environment have changed, it makes sense that they would want to know if they would be believed within the new situation. This would help them to check whether their past experience was normal and acceptable, but also make them feel safer. I described one example of this in an earlier chapter, where the child had exaggerated an incident in which they were smacked, having already told a somewhat skewed tale about being deprived. Another example occurred in my therapy work.

CASE EXAMPLE: *Guilty or not guilty?*
I worked with a 12-year-old called Saranya who had some developmental delay. She had been removed from her family of origin after chronic neglect. The foster carers told me that they felt she 'carried a heavy burden' and had never talked about her experiences in the birth family. Because her spoken language was not very good, I offered some play-based sessions. She soon established a pattern of setting up a court in the playroom, with various cuddly toys playing the victim, the perpetrator and the judge. Over many sessions she explored whether the victim's disclosure being believed or disbelieved, the perpetrator denying or accepting the charge (and whether or not he said sorry), and the judge finding the defendant guilty or not guilty, had an impact on whether or not the event really happened and how the victim felt about it.

When she established that I believed the victim was the only person who really knew what happened, regardless of what the perpetrator or judge said, she was able to begin to disclose sexual abuse from her birth father. It seemed he had confused her with repeated denials that this had happened, an apology that he said undid everything that came before it, and the persuasive idea that no one would believe her if she disclosed but he denied it. Sadly, but not atypically in my experience, she was not able to make the disclosures clearly enough in a police interview set up for achieving best evidence, and no charges were ever pressed for her to test what the real result would have been in court.

CHAPTER 18

Patterns That Suck Us In

We all have certain patterns that we repeat over and over again. Some of these are helpful patterns, like how to make the right body movements to swim or cycle or drive the car, or how to comfort a crying baby. However, sometimes we repeat patterns that are less helpful. We end up feeling frustrated and angry, but we can't seem to help ourselves. For example, some people have had experiences of being criticised and made to feel small by others who are trying to make themselves feel clever or powerful. They might then respond in a much stronger way to perceived criticism, either by feeling small and shamed or by trying to assert that they are powerful or superior. They might continue to do this even if the results are unhelpful, for example in response to feedback from a superior in the work place.

These patterns have then become 'traps' in the language of Dr Anthony Ryle, who developed a form of therapy to work with people with very entrenched problems in relating to others,[55] such as getting fixed ideas about a 'false choice', where we think that we have to always be at one extreme of a particular concept. For example, I might think that 'either I give in and please others but feel taken advantage of or I refuse and everybody hates me' or 'either

---

55　His Cognitive Analytic Therapy is particularly helpful for people with Personality Disorder, which I would view as 'attachment disorder grown up' in that it is a pattern of relating to others developed through the long-term impact of chronic trauma, abuse and neglect.

I am critical and superior or I feel criticised and worthless.'
These roles might be learnt from how we interact with a
parent, where one side of the choice is how the parent
behaved and the other how the child behaved.

I find it useful to think about the reciprocal roles that
take place between a parent and a child. These are patterns
where each side is a response to the other and reinforces the
other (see Doodle 24). If a child has learnt that most of the
time they are ignored and have to be self-sufficient (but feel
non-existent), then this would be an example pair. The child
makes no demands on the parent and so the parent provides
nothing for the child, but the child has learnt to make
no demands because the parent is not available to make
demands of, and is not providing any input. Similarly the
child may learn to be very provocative and demanding so
that this definitely gets a response, but the response may be
very negative and punitive because the parent is not able to
be child-centred and simply sees the child as being naughty.

A child may learn to take up a role that gets some
positive feedback, whether by meeting the adult's needs
(including by colluding with sexual abuse), or creating guilt
or sympathy by being ill, injured or babyish. The child may
not have learnt the pattern most prevalent in families where
secure attachment is the norm, whereby they are able to
express needs directly, and receive unconditional love and
support. So, when they experience someone being loving,
they wonder which of their established patterns it fits into
– is the adult wanting something in return, or do they feel
guilty or sorry for them? If this unfamiliar pattern feels
too threatening they might do something to return to their
familiar patterns by behaving in a way that is provocative
and invites punishment, or by ignoring and rejecting the
approach the way their neglectful parent would. As you

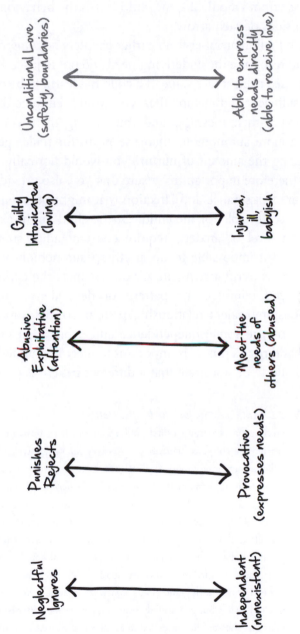

Neglectful
Ignores
⟷
Independent
(nonexistent)

Punishes
Rejects
⟷
Provocative
(expresses needs)

Abusive
Exploitative
(attention)
⟷
Meet the
needs of
others (abused)

Guilty
Intoxicated
(loving)
⟷
Injured,
ill,
babyish

Unconditional Love
(safety, boundaries)
⟷
Able to express
needs directly
(able to receive love)

DOODLE 24

can see from Doodle 24, the child learns the behaviours on
both sides of each arrow.

You will remember from earlier chapters how important
it is to recognise the underlying need and not to just take the
expressed need at face value. If a child has learnt to be overly
self-sufficient and mature, then you would reinforce this by
following their messages and thus letting them continue
to be more autonomous than the norm for their age and
reducing the amount of nurture you would normally offer.
It is therefore important to ensure that you also provide the
nurture, reassurance and affection that might be unfamiliar
or uncomfortable for the child. Or the child might express
a high level of anxiety, require constant adult attention
and find it impossible to do anything autonomously as if
the idea is terrifying. Again, if you just meet the expressed
need you reinforce the pattern of dependence and an
anxious ambivalent relationship pattern, so it is important
to encourage some independence and exploration even if
the child resists this. It is important to meet that underlying
need and to demonstrate that a different pattern is possible.

CASE EXAMPLE: Who has the biggest teeth?
I worked with a care leaver called Jamila who had been through a large
number of different placements. She had a very chaotic lifestyle, with lots
of conflict in her social group, and was 'couch surfing' from one address
to another with no permanent accommodation of her own. Jamila had a
string of relationships with males involved in crime and violence, many of
whom treated her very badly. She was often the victim of domestic violence
and assaults, and twice of rape. She had also claimed to be pregnant several
times, with various stories about lost pregnancies, although only one
miscarriage was recorded in her medical notes.

When I worked with Jamila, I was somewhat overwhelmed by the level
of chaos in her life, but it gradually began to form some patterns. One of
these was that she was often attracted to a man she perceived as being fierce

enough to fend off the previous man, once they had fallen out. We talked about how in her world the ideal man was a wolf who had big sharp teeth to fend off danger from others, but the risk was that he would turn his teeth on her. She felt that she mitigated this risk by claiming to be pregnant.

As we worked together I was able to identify that this pattern had been formed early in her life. There had been a number of violent and sexually abusive men around during her childhood, and she had learnt that she could trade sex for protection from the physical aggression that felt like a constant risk. Whenever anyone was kind to her (even a parent figure), she assumed that they were only attracted to her as a potential sexual partner, and her sexualised response had made a lot of carers very uncomfortable and contributed to her high rate of placement breakdown.

When I engaged in therapy with her, we explicitly talked about the nature of this new relationship for her, and how I was going to act as a safe, non-sexual, non-threatening person to prove that such a relationship existed. She found it very hard to fit that into her template of relationship patterns. At times she appeared to try to provoke me into rejecting her by being insulting or refusing to do the work we had agreed. I came away from sessions feeling a whole range of emotions including sympathy, guilt, frustration and anger. The latter was certainly not typical of my feelings towards a vulnerable young woman, but was something she was able to provoke even in someone as placid as me, due to her recurrent experiences of relating to people who were aggressive.

Just as I have related in my own experience above, a lot of non-birth-parent carers tell me that they sometimes feel very angry or uncomfortable with the child and don't know where these feelings came from. They are often highly self-critical about these feelings (for example crying and telling me that they didn't adopt a child to yell at him or have thoughts of shaking or hitting him). This is the hallmark of being sucked into someone else's patterns. You end up enacting the opposite pole of the reciprocal role brought from the child's history,[56] that is, you feel drawn to react to how the child is expecting you to react, which is based on their family of origin. This is very uncomfortable because such abusive ways of interacting are not in our own repertoire.

In those situations I find it useful to 'name the game and change the game'. That is, to say something like, 'I think you are trying to make me feel angry with you. Let's go and do something different.' However, it can be really difficult to recognise the patterns before you are completely sucked into playing them out.

I find the poem *Holes: Autobiography in Five Short Chapters* by Portia Nelson helpful in this regard. In the first verse she walks down a road and falls into a hole, which is scary and takes a long time to get out of. In the next verse she walks down the road and falls into the hole, which is familiar and easier to get out of. In the third verse she walks down the road, sees the hole coming but falls in it anyway, but is able to get out quickly. In the fourth verse she walks down the road, sees the hole and is able to walk around it. In the fifth verse she walks down a different road. This poem reminds us that if we hit a challenge that we can't overcome immediately, it might take some time to tackle. We first need to recognise being in it and practise getting out of it quickly before we can learn to see it coming and avoid it altogether.

✎ Activity: Mapping out patterns

↳ You may find that your child repeats and repeats certain patterns, despite them not leading to a successful outcome. You may be able to map out their patterns with the reciprocal role pairs like I have illustrated in Doodle 24. If you are able

---

56   Non-birth-parents can feel drawn to react how the child is expecting them to react. See Archer and Gordon (2006).

to recognise patterns whilst they are playing out, this would be a good time to use empathy to link their past experiences and what they have learnt to the current problems. It can also be an opportunity to use a story to highlight the pattern and make it safe to talk about, so that you can point out when it is happening and help the child to see it coming.

↓ It may be that when you map out the patterns, you find you are unwittingly being drawn into them. This is a very good thing to know! I remember when I first started mapping some of my therapy relationships in my supervision and realising there were patterns that had sucked me in. That was quite a revelation, but it was really helpful to learn, as it meant I could be aware of the processes and reflect them to the person I was working with. So, don't be ashamed. Simply work out how you are going to react differently in future and start to actively tackle the problem.

USING YOUR SUPPORT NETWORK

The other important thing to do is to recognise when you need outside help. I find that a lot of adoptive and foster parents feel like they have had to prove themselves so much that they should not show signs of weakness. However, it is actually a strength to recognise when you need some support, and much preferable to saying, 'It's fine, it's fine, it's fine, it's broken' when it comes to professionals' understanding of how the placement is going. We would much rather meet a caregiver who is able to identify difficulties early in the process so that we can provide support to tackle them, than to wait until they are overwhelming and risking the placement breaking down. If you think back to the tug of war doodles, it is important to recognise when you are being pulled out of your secure base, or when you have extra life stresses going on which don't relate to the child which might reduce your resources (e.g. problems with your relationship, health, employment, finances, mental health, the additional needs of dependents, etc.). Hopefully some professional support or personal therapy can help you to stay in the secure pattern yourself, and feel well-informed and understood when it comes to the needs of your child.

It is also useful to remember that hearing about a child's traumatic experiences can cause you what is known as secondary trauma. If you care about a child and hear about the awful things that they have been through, and can picture scenes of abuse or violence, then this is naturally going to be upsetting and can stay with you for a long time. Kate Cairns has written a lot about the impact of secondary trauma, and believes it is one of the hardest aspects to being a non-birth-parent carer. I find it somewhat ironic that the people we most want to step forward as adoptive and foster parents are those who can really hold the child in mind and offer them sincere empathy, but it is these very qualities that make them susceptible to being traumatised by the stories the child brings from their past experiences. As a therapist I have many support networks in place to help me to deal with those images and feelings, but in your personal life they can really cause distress that you don't have a means to process. Again, if talking to your personal and professional support network is not sufficient, I would really recommend seeking out some personal therapy in this situation.

It might also be that you want to share information about the attachment difficulties your child is experiencing with other members of the family, your friends, the child's school or nursery, or other sections of your network. This is entirely appropriate and will mean that you can all support each other and work in a consistent way, so that the child gains maximum benefit. You might like to lend them this book!

CHAPTER 19

Heroes

As an end note, I'd like to think about what makes a hero. It is an activity that I get people to think about in my groups. I ask participants to think of someone or something from history or the present, reality or fiction, that has qualities that they admire. This might be a character from a book, film or game, a sportsperson, a politician or activist, a community leader, a member of their family or any other character or individual.

Reflection: Heroes
Have a think about your own personal heroes. What qualities do they possess? What makes them stand out from the norm? What do you admire about them?

When we combine all our responses to these questions in the group, regardless of who people have chosen as heroes, we normally end up with a spider diagram like Doodle 25. Then I ask people to consider which of these qualities they can identify in themselves and/or their child. I hope you will be able to recognise quite a few. Foster and adoptive parents are often amazingly selfless, resilient, persistent, compassionate people who advocate for the needs of their children. It takes an amazing person to choose to care for a child who has experienced abuse and neglect, and to stand by them when their behaviour is challenging, but the majority of parents I have worked with are too humble to acknowledge this.

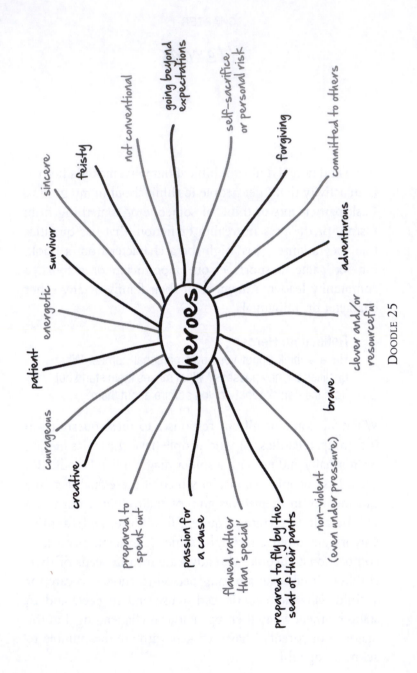

heroes

- sincere
- feisty
- not conventional
- going beyond expectations
- self-sacrifice or personal risk
- forgiving
- committed to others
- adventurous
- clever and/or resourceful
- brave
- non-violent (even under pressure)
- prepared to fly by the seat of their pants
- flawed rather than 'special'
- passion for a cause
- prepared to speak out
- creative
- courageous
- patient
- energetic
- survivor

DOODLE 25

I previously mentioned an animation by Hayao Miyazaki. Well, one of the things that makes me love his work is his belief that 'a hero is an ordinary person who rises to a challenge'. I strongly agree with that definition, and on that basis I've met a lot of heroes in my groups and clinics!

The Impact of Poor Early Care

The type of attachment relationship formed between a parent and their infant has a powerful influence on the potential health, social and economic opportunities of that child throughout their lifetime. This is particularly remarkable given that the template for a child's attachment relationship style is largely determined before the age of two. Attachment style has an impact on a huge variety of psychosocial outcomes, including academic achievements, marital satisfaction, likelihood of criminal involvement, mental health and quality of relationship with their own children (Sainsbury Centre for Mental Health 2009). Correlations are also evidenced between childhood trauma and the incidence of chronic diseases in adulthood, and their impact on functioning and healthcare uptake (Feeney 2000; Raque-Bogdan *et al.* 2011). For example, attachment style is shown to influence health outcomes in childhood infections and asthma, cancer and diabetes (Bazzazian and Besharat 2012; Cicero *et al.* 2009; Ciechanowski *et al.* 2004; Mäntymaa *et al.* 2003; Tacon 2003; Tacon, Caldera and Bell 2001).

There is complex interplay between a baby's experiences and their neurological development, with optimal development being more likely where a parent is physically and psychologically available, attuned to the infant's needs and able to hold that child in mind. It is sensitive interaction with the caregiver that teaches a child to regulate their physiological arousal level, to recognise their emotions and to 'mentalise' or understand the nature of minds (Meins *et al.* 1998). Early attachment experiences have been shown to influence brain development, with early exposure to trauma and a lack of nurture leading to a state of heightened physiological arousal and differences in cortisol production (Bruce *et al.* 2009; Gunnar and Vazquez 2001). This increased readiness for fight or flight can show in anxious or aggressive behaviour, and may mean the child is less effective at empathy, emotional regulation and executive functions like planning and anticipating the effect of behaviour. This can lead to problems in the family and/or school (which may be conceptualised as internal to the child, e.g. ADHD) and lead to referrals to educational support services and CAMHS. Early life stress confers risk for later psychopathology such as anxiety, depression, post-traumatic stress, substance misuse and psychosis (Mueller *et al.* 2010). When attachment relationships or the early environment are so dysfunctional that the child is removed into care this picture is exaggerated further still. Care leavers are 50 times more likely to go to prison, 88 times more likely to be involved in drug use and 60 times more likely to be homeless than people not looked after (Barnardo's *et al.* 2000).

Maternal factors are a huge influence on the attachment style of the infant, with depression, stress and social or partner support being particularly influential (Atkinson *et al.* 2000; Halligan *et al.* 2007). Interventions which help mothers to improve their mental health, reduce stress, and increase mentalisation and self-compassion have been shown to improve the attachment and outcomes for their infants (Cree 2010; Neff and McGehee 2010). Such early interventions have been shown to be highly cost effective and to make lasting changes for the life outcomes of the next generation (Sainsbury Centre for Mental Health 2009).

APPENDIX REFERENCES

Atkinson, L., Paglia, A., Coolbear, J., Niccols, A., Parker, K., and Guger. S. (2000) 'Attachment security: A meta-analysis of maternal mental health correlates.' *Clinical Psychology Review 20*, 8, 1019–1040.

Barnardo's, Child Poverty Action Group, Children in Wales, The Children's Society, NSPCC, and SCF (2000) *Wales' Children, Our Future – A Manifesto.*

Bazzazian, S., and Besharat, M. (2012) 'An explanatory model of adjustment to type I diabetes based on attachment, coping, and self-regulation theories.' *Psychology, Health & Medicine 17*, 1, 47–58.

Bruce, J., Fisher, P.A., Pears, K.C., and Levine, S. (2009) 'Morning cortisol levels in preschool-aged foster children: Differential effects of maltreatment type.' *Developmental Psychobiology 51*, 1, 14–23.

Cicero, V., Lo Coco, G., Gullo, S., and Lo Verso, G. (2009) 'The role of attachment dimensions and perceived social support in predicting adjustment to cancer.' *Psycho-Oncology 18*, 10, 1045–1052.

Ciechanowski, P., Russo, J., Katon, W., Von Korff, M., *et al.* (2004) 'Influence of patient attachment style on self-care and outcomes in diabetes.' *Psychosomatic Medicine 66*, 5, 720–728.

Cree, M. (2010) 'Compassion focused therapy with perinatal and mother–infant distress.' *International Journal of Cognitive Therapy 3, Special Section: Compassion Focused Therapy*, 159–171.

Feeney, J.A. (2000) 'Implications of attachment style for patterns of health and illness.' *Child: Care, Health and Development 26*, 4, 277–288.

Gunnar, M.R., and Vazquez, D.M. (2001) 'Low cortisol and a flattening of expected daytime rhythm: Potential indices of risk in human development.' *Development and Psychopathology 13*, 515–538.

Halligan, S.L., Murray, L., Martin, C., and Cooper, P.J. (2007) 'Maternal depression and psychiatric outcomes in adolescent offspring: A 13-year longitudinal study.' *Journal of Affective Disorders 97*, 145–154.

Mäntymaa, M., Puura, K., Luoma, I., Salmelin, R., *et al.* (2003) 'Infant–mother interaction as a predictor of child's chronic health problems.' *Child Care, Health and Development 29*, 3, 181–191.

Meins, E., Fernyhough, C., Russell, J., and Clark-Carter, D. (1998) 'Security of attachment as a predictor of symbolic and mentalising abilities: A longitudinal study.' *Social Development 7*, 1, 1–24.

Mueller, S., Maheu, F., Dozier, M., Peloso, E., *et al.* (2010) 'Early-life stress is associated with impairment in cognitive control in adolescence: an fMRI study.' *Neuropsychologia 48*, 3037–3044.

Neff, K., and McGehee, P. (2010) 'Self-compassion and psychological resilience among adolescents and young adults.' *Self and Identity 9*, 3, 225–240.

Raque-Bogdan, T.L., Ericson, S.K., Jackson, J., Martin, H.M., and Bryan, N.A. (2011) 'Attachment and mental and physical health: Self-compassion and mattering as mediators.' *Journal of Counselling Psychology 58*, 2, 272–278.

Sainsbury Centre for Mental Health (2009) *The chance of a lifetime: Preventing early conduct problems and reducing crime.* Available at www.scmh.org.uk/pdfs/chance_of_a_lifetime.pdf, accessed on 11 September 2012. See also www.wsipp.wa.gov/rptfiles/04-07-3901.pdf, accessed on 11 September 2012.

Tacon, A. (2003) 'Attachment experiences in women with breast cancer.' *Family & Community Health 26*, 2, 147–156.

Tacon, A., Caldera, Y., and Bell, N. (2001) 'Attachment style, emotional control, and breast cancer.' *Families, Systems, & Health 19*, 3, 319–326.

Glossary

Abuse Acts that cause harm to another person, whether this be emotional, sexual or physical

ADHD Attention deficit hyperactivity disorder, diagnosis given where children are overactive and/or impulsive and/or unable to concentrate

Adoption A permanent placement with a new family where one or more adults take on the legal rights of being the child's parent

Adrenalin A chemical messenger preparing the body for activity

Ambivalent A pattern of insecure attachment where the child becomes clingy and is not able to show age-appropriate autonomy because they do not feel reassured enough

Amygdala An almond-shaped nodule in the inner section of the brain concerned with more primitive functions such as sensing threat

Arousal How ready your body is for fight or flight

ASC Autism spectrum conditions, a range of presentations of varying severity related to autism, typically involving difficulties with social skills, communication and the flexibility of thinking

ASD Autistic spectrum disorder, now known as ASC

Asperger's Syndrome An ASC in which the person does not have learning disability or any language delay and the difficulties may be less marked than classical autism

Attachment The relationship a child has with the main caregiver, and the template this gives them for how relationships work

Attachment disorder A diagnostic label given if a child struggles to form a healthy relationship with new carers because of past abuse and/or neglect

Attunement Being able to hold someone else in mind, pick up their signals in a sensitive way and care about their experience

Avoidant A pattern of insecure attachment where the child avoids relying on anyone else, or showing any feelings; they may act as if they are tough and self-sufficient

Black out Lose consciousness

Boundaries Consistent and clear rules

CAMHS Child and Adolescent Mental Health Service, a UK acronym for a team of professionals in each local area who work with children's mental health issues as part of the NHS

Care Living in public care, in a foster family or residential home, rather than family of origin

Caregiver A parent, adoptive parent, foster carer or person who takes on the primary care of a child

CAT Cognitive Analytic Therapy, a model of therapy developed by Anthony Ryle to address dysfunctional relationship patterns and personality disorders

CBT Cognitive Behaviour Therapy, a very well evidenced model of therapy with work on changing thoughts, feelings and behaviours, often using small experiments to test assumptions

Chaotic Unpredictable to the point of feeling unsafe

Chronic Developmental Trauma A diagnostic category related to post-traumatic stress disorder proposed by van der Kolk for children who were exposed to chaotic and harmful care for a prolonged period of time

Claiming narrative A story in which the caregiver tells the child about the care they deserved and how they would have provided this

Clinical psychologist A term normally indicative of being a licensed professional with expertise in mental health and therapy, with training to doctoral level

Co-regulate Help the child to set their level of arousal to an appropriate level by matching the caregiver's

Consequences Positive and negative things that we do in response to what the child does, when trying to shape their behaviour

Cortisol A chemical messenger in the brain and nervous system related to sensing threat

DBT Dialectical Behaviour Therapy, a model of therapy developed by Marsha Linehan to address chronic patterns of dysfunction including self-harm and inability to tolerate distress

DDP Dyadic Developmental Psychotherapy, a parent–child therapy developed by Dan Hughes, to help enhance the attachment relationship and allow the child to develop along a more positive trajectory

Developmental level Where the child is up to in their development (note that this may not match their chronological age)

Disorganised A category of insecure attachment where the caregiver has been chaotic and/or harmful and no single (organised) strategy of relationship pattern has worked to meet the child's needs

Domestic violence Verbal, physical or sexual violence against a family member or someone living or staying within the same household

Dopamine A chemical messenger in the brain associated with action and rewards

Dyspraxia Difficulty in getting the brain to coordinate and sequence body movements, which typically shows as clumsiness and needing active concentration to complete any motor activity

Dysregulation A state in which a person's emotions are out of their control and their body is in a state of increased arousal

Earned secure A category of adult attachment where the person has been able to reflect on their poor early care experiences and learn a healthier template for relating to other people. Research shows that parents within this category do almost as well with their children as those whose childhoods put them in the secure category

Empathy The ability to understand how other people feel

Expressed need What is communicated directly

Fight, flight, freeze The ways a child learns to behave when there is a threat; they can either attempt to fight it off physically, to run away from it, or to become still and watchful until the threat has passed

Formulation A map of the contributing factors which influence someone's presentation, normally including the predisposing risk factors, the maintenance cycles and the symptoms and behaviours that are produced as a result

Foster carer Someone who cares for a child (normally one that is not blood related or previously known to them) but has not been legally awarded the full rights of a parent, which usually means a social worker will need to be involved in making all major decisions about the child

'Good enough' parent A legal phrase used to describe a parent who is adequate and does not cause their child to be harmed due to their care

High functioning autism An ASC in which the person is of above average intelligence, which has a better prognosis for independent living in adulthood than classical autism

Hyperarousal Being constantly in a state of increased readiness for fight or flight

Hyperkinetic disorder The British (International Classification of Diseases) equivalent of the American (Diagnostic and Statistical Manual) diagnostic category of ADHD, although the criteria are said to be more stringent

Innate Something you are born with

Insecure A less healthy relationship with a caregiver who is not consistently available and attuned

Intuitive Done by instinct

Kinship A placement with someone known to the child, such as a member of their extended family (e.g. an uncle or aunt or grandparent) or their wider network (e.g. a neighbour or teacher or family friend)

Learned secure See Earned secure

Learning difficulty A specific area of difficulty in learning, such as dyslexia

Learning disability Having an IQ below 70 (which is in the bottom 2% of the population) and similar levels of difficulty with activities of daily living. This is considered to be a form of disability. Learning disability is a British term equivalent to intellectual/developmental disability in the USA, which supersedes terms which are considered stigmatising like 'mental handicap' (UK) or 'mental retardation' (USA)

Looked after In public care

Maltreatment Being treated badly

Narrative Story

Neglect Not doing the things necessary to ensure the safe and healthy development of a child (e.g. keeping the environment clean, providing regular food, meeting medical needs, accessing education and appropriate social experiences)

Neurodevelopmental Describes conditions that are to do with the way the brain develops

Nurture Attuned loving care which meets the emotional and psychological needs of the child

Organised Used to describe an insecure attachment pattern that is applied consistently and does not reach the threshold of being unusual or harmful enough to cause concern

Oxytocin A chemical messenger associated with love, sex, skin contact and feeling safe and soothed

Paradoxical Doing the opposite of what is expected

Plastic Able to change

Prefrontal cortex The area of the brain above the eyes, associated with self-monitoring, planning, sequencing, understanding cause and effect, empathy and other sophisticated thought patterns underlying social skills

Psychiatrist A medical doctor specialising in mental health

Psychologist Someone highly trained in mental health and therapy, but who is not medically qualified

Quasi-autistic A term for children who appear autistic due to severe and chronic neglect

Reassurance A message that you are okay, and help to regulate and feel confident to go out and explore once again

Reflection Actively thinking about things in a different way

Reflective capacity The degree to which we are able to think about our experiences, thoughts, feelings, behaviours and patterns of relating to others

Regulate Return the level of arousal to a resting state

Resilience Ability to cope with stress and challenges

Schema A belief about the fundamental nature of yourself, the world and other people

Secure A healthy relationship with an attuned and predictable caregiver

Secure base A person who is able to provide attunement and reassurance and helps you to regulate

Self-image The way we understand ourselves and how good we feel about who we are

Self-regulate Being in control of your own emotions and able to soothe yourself when distressed so that you do not stay in too high a state of arousal for too long

Sensory integration A process promoted by occupational therapists for helping children to organise sensory information

Shame A belief that you are inherently flawed, bad or unlovable

Strange situation A task used to study the relationship between infants and their parents. It involves the parent leaving the room and returning and looking at the infant's reaction to the separation and reunion

Theory of mind A term used to refer to having a model of how minds work, which allows a person to guess the thoughts and feelings of another person and better understand their behaviour

Theraplay A therapy technique developed by Ann Jernberg and Phyllis Booth within the Head Start scheme in America, in which the parent and child engage in playful interactions to enhance attachment, self-esteem, trust in others and joy within their relationship

Transgenerational Passing from one generation to the next, grandparent to parent to child

Trauma Significant negative experiences which caused the child to fear for their safety

Trigger Any source of stress or reminder of past experiences that can set off patterns of thoughts, feelings or behaviours

Unconscious Outside of the person's awareness, not deliberate

Underlying need A need that is not communicated directly

References

Ainsworth, M.D.S., Blehar, M.C., Waters, E., and Wall, S. (1978) *Patterns of Attachment: A Psychological Study of the Strange Situation*. Hillsdale, NJ: Earlbaum.

Appleyard, K., and Osofsky, J.D. (2003) 'Parenting after trauma: supporting parents and caregivers in the treatment of children impacted by violence.' *Infant Mental Health Journal 24*, 2, 111–125.

Archer, C., and Gordon, C. (2006) *New Families, Old Scripts: A Guide to the Language of Trauma and Attachment in Adoptive Families*. London: Jessica Kingsley Publishers.

Banyard, V.L., Rozelle, D., and Englund, D.W. (2001) 'Parenting the traumatized child: Attending to the needs of nonoffending caregivers.' *Psychotherapy: Theory, Research, Practice, Training 38*, 1, 74–87.

Bhreathnach, E. (2006) *Parent–Child Engagement, a Co-Regulation Process*. Keynote address at the third National Conference for Occupational Therapists in Child and Adolescent Mental Health, Northampton. Available at www.sensoryattachmentintervention.com/Documents/CAMHS%20Paperrws.doc, accessed on 12 September 2012.

Burns, L.H. (1990) An exploratory study of perceptions of parenting after infertility. *Family Systems Medicine 8*, 2, 177–189.

Caltabiano, M., and Thorpe, R. (2007) 'Attachment style of foster carers and caregiving role performance.' *Child Care in Practice 13*, 12, 137–148.

Carlson, V., Cicchetti, D., Barnett, D., and Braunwald, K. (1989) 'Disorganized/disoriented attachment relationships in maltreated infants.' *Developmental Psychology 25*, 4, 525–531.

Carpenter, G.L., and Stacks, A.M. (2009) 'Developmental effects of exposure to intimate partner violence in early childhood: A review of the literature.' *Child and Youth Services Review 31*, 8, 831–839.

Cleaver, H., Unell, I., and Aldgate, J. (1999) *Children's Needs – Parenting Capacity: The Impact of Parental Mental Illness, Problem Alcohol and Drug Use, and Domestic Violence on Children's Development*. London: The Stationery Office.

Cozolino, L. (2002) *The Neuroscience of Psychotherapy: Building and Rebuilding the Human Brain*. New York: W.W. Norton.

Crittenden, P.M. (1997) 'Truth, error, omission, distortion and deception: The application of attachment theory to the assessment and treatment of psychological disorder.' In S.M.C. Dollinger and L.F. Dilalla (eds), *Assessment and Intervention Across the Lifespan*. Hillsdale, NJ: Erlbaum.

Davis-Kean, P.E. (2005) 'The influence of parent education and family income on child achievement: The indirect role of parental expectations and the home environment.' *Journal of Family Psychology 19*, 2, 294–304.

Dodge, K.A., Bates, J.E., and Pettit, G.S. (1990) 'Mechanisms in the cycle of violence.' *Science 250*, 1678–1683.

Dozier, M., Lindheim, O., and Ackerman, J. (2005) 'Attachment and biobehavioral catchup.' In L. Berlin, Y. Ziv, L. Amaya-Jackson and M.T. Greenberg (eds), *Enhancing Early Attachments*. New York: Guilford Press.

Dozier, M., Higley, E., Albus, K., and Nutter, A. (2002) 'Intervening with foster infants' caregivers.' *Infant Mental Health Journal 25*, 541–554.

Felitti, V.J., Anda, R.F., Nordenberg, D., Williamson, D.F., Spitz, A.M., and Edwards, V. (1998) 'Relationship of childhood abuse and household dysfunction to many of the leading causes of death in adults. The Adverse Childhood Experiences (ACE) Study.' *American Journal of Preventive Medicine 14*, 245–258.

Fonagy, P., Steele, H., and Steele, M. (1991) 'Maternal representations of attachment during pregnancy predict the organization of infant–mother attachment at one year of age.' *Child Development 62*, 891–905.

Fonagy, P., Steele, M., Steele, H., Higgitt, A., and Target, M. (1994) 'The Emanuel Miller Memorial Lecture 1992: The theory and practice of resilience.' *Journal of Child Psychology and Psychiatry 35*, 2, 231–257.

Ford, T., Vostanis, P., Meltzer, H., and Goodman, R. (2007) 'Psychiatric disorder among British children looked after by local authorities: Comparison with children living in private households.' *British Journal of Psychiatry 190*, 4, 319–325.

Gass, K., Jenkins, J., and Dunn, J. (2007) 'Are sibling relationships protective? A longitudinal study.' *Journal of Child Psychology and Psychiatry 48*, 2, 167–175.

Glaser, D. (2001) 'Child abuse and neglect and the brain – A review.' *Journal of Child Psychology and Psychiatry and Allied Disciplines 41*, 1, 97–116.

Golding, K. (2008) *Nurturing Attachments: Supporting Children Who Are Fostered or Adopted.* London: Jessica Kingsley Publishers.

Grandin, T. (2006) *Thinking in Pictures.* London: Bloomsbury.

Grandin, T. (2008) *The Way I See It: A Personal Look at Autism and Asperger's.* Arlington, TX: Future Horizons.

Grandin, T., and Scariano, M.M. (2005) *Emergence: Labelled Autistic.* New York: Warner.

Hart, R., and McMahon, C.A. (2006) 'Mood state and psychological adjustment to pregnancy.' *Archives of Women's Mental Health 9*, 6, 329–337.

Hoghughi, M., and Speight, A.N.P. (1998) 'Good enough parenting for all children – A strategy for a healthier society.' *Archives of Disease in Childhood 78*, 4, 293–296.

Holmes, B., and Silver, M. (2010) 'Managing behaviour with attachment in mind.' *Adoption and Fostering Journal 34*, 1, 65–76.

Howard, L.M., Kumar, R., and Thornicroft, G. (2001) 'Psychosocial characteristics and needs of mothers with psychotic disorders.' *British Journal of Psychiatry 178*, 5, 427–432.

Howe, D. (2005) *Child Abuse and Neglect: Attachment, Development and Intervention.* Basingstoke: Palgrave Macmillan.

Hughes, D.A. (2006a) *Building the Bonds of Attachment: Awakening Love in Deeply Troubled Children* [DVD]. Available at www.danielhughes.org/html/booksdvd.html, accessed on 11 September 2012.

Hughes, D.A. (2006b) *Building the Bonds of Attachment: Awakening Love in Deeply Troubled Children.* Lanham, MD: Jason Aronson.

Hughes, D.A. (2007) *Attachment-focused family therapy.* New York: W.W. Norton.

Kaniuk, J., Steele, M., and Hodges, J. (2004) 'Report on a longitudinal research project, exploring the development of attachments between older, hard-to-place children and their adopters over the first two years of placement.' *Adoption & Fostering Journal 28*, 2, 61–67.

Lacher, D., Nichols, T., Nichols, M., and May, J.C. (2012) *Connecting With Kids Through Stories: Using Narratives to Facilitate Attachment in Adopted Children* [second edition]. London: Jessica Kingsley Publishers.

Lichtenstein Phelps, J., Belsky, J., and Crnic, K. (1998) 'Earned security, daily stress and parenting: A comparison of five alternative models.' *Development and Psychopathology 10*, 1, 21–38. Available at http://journals.cambridge.org/action/displayAbstract;jsessionid=34993D7997A67322F0 8283EE816068A0.journals?fromPage=online&aid=43529, accessed on 11 September 2012.

McMahon, C.A., Tennant, C., Ungerer, J., and Saunders, D. (1999) 'Don't count your chickens: A comparative study of the experience of pregnancy after IVF conception.' *Journal of Reproductive and Infant Psychology 17*, 4, 345–356.

Matsueda, R.L. (1992) 'Reflected appraisals, parental labelling, and delinquency: Specifying a Symbolic Interactionist Theory.' *American Journal of Sociology 97*, 6, 1577–1611.

Mills, K. (1998) *Something Better for my Children: The History and People of Head Start.* New York: Dutton.

Nummenmaa, L., Glerean, E., Viinikainen, M., Jääskeläinen, I.P., Hari, R., and Sams, M. (2012) 'Emotions promote social interaction by synchronizing brain activity across individuals.' *Proceedings of the National Academy of Sciences of the United States of America 109*, 24, 9599–9604.

O'Connor, T.G., Heron, J., Golding, J., Beveridge, M., and Glover, V. (2002) 'Maternal antenatal anxiety and children's behavioural/emotional problems at 4 years: Report from the Avon Longitudinal Study of Parents and Children.' *The British Journal of Psychiatry 180*, 6, 502–508.

Read, J., van Os, J., Morrison, A.P., and Ross, C.A. (2005) 'Childhood trauma, psychosis and schizophrenia: A literature review with theoretical and clinical implications.' *Acta Psychiatrica Scandinavica 112*, 5, 330–350.

Reder, P., and Lucey, C. (2000) *Assessment of Parenting: Psychiatric and Psychological Contributions.* London and New York: Routledge.

Rosenthal, R., and Jacobson, L. (1968) 'Pygmalion in the classroom.' *The Urban Review 3*, 1, 16–20.

Rothman, B.K. (1986) *The Tentative Pregnancy.* New York: Penguin.

Roy, P., Rutter, M., and Pickles, A. (2004) 'Institutional care: Associations between overactivity and lack of selectivity in social relationships.' *Journal of Child Psychology and Psychiatry 45*, 4, 866–873.

Rutter, M., Kreppner, J., Croft, C., Murin, M., *et al.* (2007) 'Early adolescent outcomes of institutionally deprived and non-deprived adoptees. III. Quasi-autism.' *Journal of Child Psychology and Psychiatry 48*, 1200–1207.

Sansone, R.A., Furukhi, S., and Wiederman, M.W. (2012) 'History of childhood trauma and disruptive behaviours in the medical setting.' *International Journal of Psychiatry in Clinical Practice 16*, 1, 68–71.

Saunders, R., Jacobvitz, D., Zaccagnino, M., Beverung, L.M., and Hazen, N. (2011) 'Pathways to earned security: the role of alternative support figures.' *Attachment and Human Development 13*, 4, 403–420.

Siegel, D.J. (2006) 'An interpersonal neurobiology approach to psychotherapy: Awareness, mirror neurons, and neural plasticity in the development of well-being.' *Psychiatric Annals 36*, 4, 248–256.

Slade, A. (2005) 'Parental reflective functioning: an introduction.' *Attachment and Human Development 7*, 3, 269–281.

Teicher, M.H., Andersen, S.L., Polcari, A., Anderson, A.M., Navalta, C.P., and Kim, D.M. (2003) 'The neurobiological consequences of early stress and childhood maltreatment.' *Neuroscience & Biobehavioral Reviews 27*, 1–2, 33–44.

Transgenerational domestic violence: www.ncbi.nlm.nih.gov/pubmed/15583508, accessed on 11 September 2012.

Tronick, E. (1986) 'Interactive mismatch and repair: Challenges to the coping infant.' *Zero to Three 6*, 1–6.

Uylings, H.B.M. (2006) 'Development of the human cortex and the concept of 'critical' or 'sensitive' periods.' *Language Learning 56*, Suppl., 59–90.

van IJzendoorn, M. (1995) 'Adult attachment representations, parental responsiveness, and infant attachment: A meta-analysis on the predictive validity of the Adult Attachment Interview.' *Psychological Bulletin 117*, 3, 387–403.

van IJzendoorn, M.H., Juffer, F., and Duyvesteyn, M.G.C. (1995) 'Breaking the intergenerational cycle of insecure attachment – A review of the effects of attachment-based interventions on maternal sensitivity and infant security.' *Journal of Child Psychology and Psychiatry and Allied Disciplines 36*, 225–248.

van IJzendoorn, M.H., Schuengel, C., and Bakermans Kranenburg, M.J. (1999) 'Disorganized attachment in early childhood: Meta-analysis of precursors, concomitants, and sequelae.' *Development and Psychopathology 11*, 225–249.

van der Kolk, B.A. (2005) 'Developmental trauma disorder: Towards a rational diagnosis for children with complex trauma histories.' *Psychiatric Annals 35*, 5, 401–408.

Wearden, A., Peters, I., Berry, K., Barrowclough, C., and Liversidge, T. (2008) 'Adult attachment, parenting experiences, and core beliefs about self and others.' *Personality and Individual Differences 44*, 5, 1246–1257.

Webster-Stratton, C. (2006) *The Incredible Years: A Guide for Parents of Children 2–8 Years Old* (revised). Toronto: The Incredible Years/Umbrella Press.

Welsh, B.C., and Farrington, D.P. (2007) 'Save children from a life of crime.' *Criminology & Public Policy 6*, 4, 871–879.

Werner, E.E., and Smith, R.S. (1992) *Overcoming the Odds: High Risk Children From Birth To Childhood.* Ithaca: Cornell University.

Winnicott, D. (1953) 'Transitional objects and transitional phenomena.' *International Journal of Psychoanalysis 34*, 89–97.

Winnicott, D.W. (1965) *The Maturational Process and the Facilitative Environment.* New York: International Universities Press.

Wolfe, D.A., Crooks, C.V., Lee, V., McIntyre-Smith, A., and Jaffe, P.G. (2003) 'The effect of children's exposure to domestic violence: A meta analysis and critique.' *Clinical Child and Family Psychology Review 6*, 3, 171–187.

Zagar, R.J., Busch, K.G., and Hughes, J.R. (2009) 'Empirical risk factors for delinquency and best treatments: where do we go from here?' *Psychological Reports 104*, 1, 279–308.

Zeanah, C.H., Keyes, A., and Settles, L. (2003) 'Attachment relationship experiences and childhood psychopathology.' *Annals of the New York Academy of Sciences 1008*, 1, 22–30. Available at www.traumacenter.org/products/pdf_files/preprint_dev_trauma_disorder.pdf, accessed on 11 September 2012.

Zigler, E., and Muenchow, S. (1994) *Head Start: The Inside Story of America's Most Successful Educational Experiment.* New York: Basic Books.

Additional Reading

Recommended books for non-birth-parent carers wishing to learn more about caring for children who have experienced trauma, abuse or neglect or who wish to improve attachment relationships.

Caroline Archer and Christine Gordon (2006) *New Families, Old Scripts: A Guide to the Language of Trauma and Attachment in Adoptive Families*. London: Jessica Kingsley Publishers.

Phyllis B. Booth and Ann M. Jernberg (2010) *Theraplay: Helping Parents and Children Build Better Relationships Through Attachment-Based Play*. San Francisco, CA: Jossey-Bass.

Adele Faber and Elaine Mazlish (2001) *How to Talk So Kids Will Listen and Listen So Kids Will Talk*. London: Piccadilly Press.

Adele Faber and Elaine Mazlish (2006) *How to Talk So Teens Will Listen and Listen So Teens Will Talk*. London: Piccadilly Press.

Sue Gerhardt (2004) *Why Love Matters: How Affection Shapes a Baby's Brain*. London: Routledge.

Kim S. Golding (2008) *Nurturing Attachments: Supporting Children Who Are Fostered or Adopted*. London: Jessica Kingsley Publishers.

Kim S. Golding and Dan A. Hughes (2012) *Creating Loving Attachments: Parenting with PACE to Nurture Confidence and Security in the Troubled Child*. London: Jessica Kingsley Publishers.

Angela Hobday, Angela Kirby and Kate Ollier (2002) *Creative Therapy for Children in New Families*. Oxford: Wiley-Blackwell.

Dan A. Hughes (2006) *Building the Bonds of Attachment: Awakening Love in Deeply Troubled Children*. Lanham, MD: Jason Aronson.

Dan A. Hughes (2007) *Principles of Attachment-Focused Parenting: Effective Strategies to Care for Children*. New York: W.W. Norton.

Dan A. Hughes, Jonathan Baylin and Daniel J. Siegel (2012) *Brain-Based Parenting: The Neuroscience of Caregiving for Health Attachment*. New York: W.W. Norton.

Denise Lacher, Todd Nichols and Joanna C. May (2005) *Connecting with Kids through Stories: Using Narratives to Facilitate Attachment in Adopted Children*. London: Jessica Kingsley Publishers.

Daniel J. Siegel (2002) *The Developing Mind: How Relationships and the Brain Interact to Shape Who We Are*. New York: Guilford Press.

Margot Sunderland (2007) *What Every Parent Needs to Know: The Incredible Effects of Love, Nurture and Play on Your Child's Development*. London: Dorling Kindersley.

Carolyn Webster-Stratton (2006) *The Incredible Years: A Guide for Parents of Children 2–8 Years Old* (revised). Toronto: The Incredible Years/Umbrella Press.

Carolyn Webster-Stratton and Martin Herbert (1994) *Troubled Families – Problem Children: Working with Parents – A Collaborative Process*. Oxford: Wiley-Blackwell.

Index